Barry Stone has been a freel...
activist for over two decade...
attributes his good physical...
which he has clocked up wh...
none too well behaved – mutts that have been a major part
of his life. Barry has a young black Labrador called Bonzo,
and when misbehaving, Asbo.

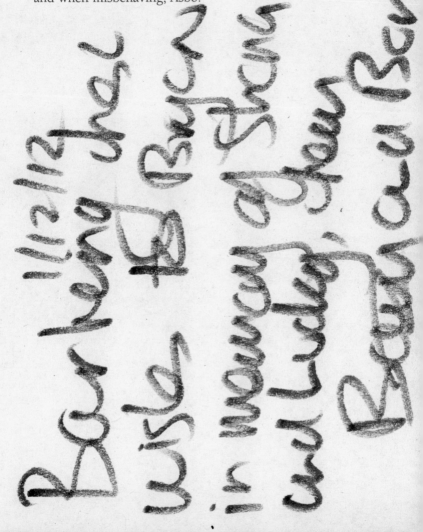

Barking Mad 11/2/12
Best Wishes to Bryn
in Memory of Shane
and Lucky, your wonderful Border...

BARKING AT WINSTON

Barry Stone

Constable • London

Constable & Robinson Ltd
55–56 Russell Square
London WC1B 4HP
www.constablerobinson.com

First published in the UK in 2010 by Zircon Press,
PO Box 812, Whitley Bay, NE26 9BX

This edition published by Constable,
an imprint of Constable & Robinson Ltd, 2011

A copy of the British Library Cataloguing in
Publication data is available from the British Library

ISBN 978-1-78033-242-0

Typeset by TW Typesetting, Plymouth, Devon

Printed and bound in the EU

3 5 7 9 10 8 6 4 2

In memory of Mum

1

It was the boiling summer of 1976. I'd been alive for one human year and unless I got lucky I wouldn't be around for another: if a dog at the municipal kennels wasn't homed by day seven the vet offed it and tossed its corpse into an incinerator thoughtlessly positioned nearby. Think how you'd feel, chatting with a neighbour in the morning, then breathing him in as his smoke wafted past in the afternoon. Still, if I'd been in the Far East, I'd probably have been served up as dinner for six.

Some of my mates made things worse for themselves: they got angry, which meant they weren't offered for rehoming. Even the most committed dog lover wasn't going to choose a mutt that might eat the baby. I admired those dogs for their sheer bravado, but pointless suicide wasn't for me: I was no hero, and a Collie Cross can usually count on a long life. I wasn't going to deny myself the remotest chance of getting one.

And, just then, 'remotest chance' was spot-on. It was the middle of August when most humans were flying off to sunnier climes, not thinking about the kennels where my week's grace was flying by. And anyone who did visit hurried past me, after a swift glance at the mange that had

1

left my back hairless and my tail looking like its blood supply had been cut off.

Would you reject a human orphan because its face had more boils than a witch's cauldron? If that's a yes – go on, be honest – you'll understand my anxiety. My red-raw appearance was such that even those Far Eastern chefs would have rejected me. For a while I considered eating my paw – if nobody else was going to relish me, I'd do it myself – but I couldn't go through with it. I had enough problems already with my terrible skin.

The big Alsatian in the next cage – Her Hoityness, I called her – told me I was a coward as she ripped at her flesh with her claws. They soon stopped that with a set of clippers, so then she started chewing her teats. Result? The vet offed her early. Tragic. I'd thought she had a lot to offer, even if she was an up-and-down sort whose female cycle apparently turned her into a part-time she-devil – and *the* dog the vet might actually have understood because she, too, had moods. Sometimes a mutt only had to look at her the wrong way to get itself dispatched straight to the kennel in the sky.

By the end of day six I'd stopped looking up at the few humans who visited (flinching at the sight of my mangy back). I knew that if my nerves settled my lovely black-and-tan coat – complemented by white hocks – would grow back, but the bitter fact was that it no longer mattered. I was all for my own survival, but I'd sunk so low I was on the verge of biting the poor kennel lad – thereby advancing my own offing.

Yet, with twenty-four hours to go, something held me in check. I'd wait for Psycho Vet to come in her own good time, syringe poised.

2

I sensed her outside my cage before I actually saw her. I was lying on the concrete with my head on my paws, eyes half closed, facing the grassy square that was framed by the four terraces of kennels.

First, I felt a rise in temperature – I put that down to the sun getting higher. Then I was aware of a familiar red mist. Sometimes it means anger but mostly it's joy. You can tell the difference right away: anger makes your coat bristle but the other gets your tail wagging like it's got a mind of its own – and my baldy tail was going like a lizard on scalding concrete. I looked up. My sore blue eyes – I had conjunctivitis as well as mange – widened. A ginger-haired woman of about fifty-five was smiling at me. Her nose was broken – that must have hurt. I wanted to lick her face.

'Aren't you an artful bugger?' she exclaimed.

I was taken aback. I was just being myself, not artful, but the red around her got brighter. She'd been playing with words.

'Aren't you an artful bugger?' she said again, bending so close that I saw my quizzically pricked ears reflected in her big green eyes.

'Yes, you are! As artful as they come!' she cooed.

Well, artful or not, if that wasn't the moment for me to

make a painful sacrifice by rolling on to my sore back, I didn't know what was. Dog-loving humans can't resist a belly that's offered for a tickle.

And since you must be wondering about the impediment of my cage, well, I saw it as an advantage: my admirer would have to crouch to put her fingers through the bars – thereby getting nice and close to me.

Instead she straightened up and stepped back. Fear jolted through me like an electric shock. Didn't she want me? My first human had had a cruel streak as wide as a river – that was why my mange came. The electric shocks he'd given me had only stopped when the human from the RSPCA took me away with him.

I kept very still so Ginger – as I'd dubbed her – wouldn't move further away, and fought the need to blink. I was convinced that my life depended on unbroken eye contact between us. My conjunctivitis was really stinging now.

'Artful bugger,' she said again – but this time in a way that suggested she was considering me as her companion. She was probably alone in the world, I thought. If I could just stop myself blinking until she'd got herself fully committed, I'd have the life of Reilly – whoever he was.

Then, beyond her legs – she was wearing trousers in the same pea-green colour as her top – I saw two pairs of tatty sandals and two more of unpolished brogues. She'd stepped back because she wanted some kids to get a good look at me. Suddenly I was in a tizz and panting hard. I jumped to my feet and started to pace – round and round my cell I went. I was seeing double – or even apparitions . . .

No, I wasn't: Ginger's kids were two quirky-looking sets of twins. Jack and Vanessa were sixteen, Craig and Rachael, a year younger. They all had a thick mop of black hair that clearly came from their dad's side of the family, and equally thick black eyebrows. Otherwise they were Ginger to a T: they had her skinny lips, Roman nose, pointy chin and honest shiny green eyes, all eight of which were glued expectantly on me. Any second now they'd see I was a repulsive freak and move on to a dog with a full fur coat.

Except that those eyes had me hurtling into a tunnel that I knew I'd never come out of: even if they didn't take me, I'd forgive them. It was love at first sight.

Maybe I *had* encountered an apparition after all. One that filled me with an iron resolve to elude Psycho Vet. I shoved my right paw through the bars of my cage and did some of what the kids and Ginger would have called whimpering – but it was their laughter that brought on my embarrassing seal wiggle (I suspect there's a splash of Labrador in me somewhere).

3

Jack, the elder lad, stepped forward and touched my paw, which was still sticking out of my cage, with the toe of his shoe. I took that to mean he wanted to make contact without getting in my face. He didn't want to pressure me, did he?

Then he spoke: 'What a frigging mess! I've seen more hair on a football!'

That was alarming – not to mention cheeky: his own hair was so thick and unruly it probably had a missing football team in it. I shoved aside the thought as I pushed the other front paw through the bars and clasped both round his ankle. It was a blatant attempt to soften his hard little heart, shameless begging, in fact, that would have enraged Her Hoityness.

He withdrew his leg, and pronounced, 'There's more mange in this cage than there was blood spilt in all of the Second World War.'

Unaware that this strange comment was an allusion to the family history, I was so annoyed I nearly growled. Hastily I blocked the sound – but too late: to my horror, my lips had parted to reveal my fangs. It was a pretty treacherous act by my own body, especially when I was fighting for my life.

To my relief, he looked at me now with respect. Most humans would have moved on to a mutt that was all charm and maybe wicked inside: nothing would make me turn on a kid. And young Jack had got me where I hurt most: I feared I was unlovable. That was what my first human had banged on about: he'd said I was ugly, worthless and should have been drowned at birth. Like he – the man who'd given me electric shocks – was my Saviour.

By now, the red mist around Ginger was mixed with colours from the kids. Green was Jack's primary shade: green for sensitivity and determination. Like a plant that surrenders when the season's up, but always comes back.

Vanessa elbowed her brother aside, serenely telling the younger twins to take no notice: until last week he hadn't even known the dates of the war. 'Still,' she added, crouching to face me and raising her voice, 'it's amazing what you can learn in a single history lesson, isn't it?'

Jack told her to get stuffed, then added for the benefit of the others that she was just rehearsing for when she grew into a big fat cow. It was an effective riposte: she was indeed carrying a bit of extra weight and went as red as a lobster quicker than you could have said, 'It's a dog's life.'

'I am not', she retorted, still facing me, 'rehearsing to be anything. Especially a cow. Fat or otherwise.'

That got me spinning, not least because the colours around my little pack were so bright I might pass out and be offed by Psycho Vet: she would have found a devastating alternative cause of the dizziness to which Vanessa was oblivious.

Suddenly she wheeled away from me to stand nose to nose with Jack, who was just half an inch taller, and therefore on the short side for a boy of his age. 'Did you hear what I said – Stick Insect?' she demanded. That wiped the smirk off his lips.

Their bickering had brought a scowl to Ginger's face, which deepened when Craig started mooing, getting up the hooter of his own twin Rachael, who said, 'Do something, Mum. Our Craig's going retard.'

Vanessa broke eye contact with Jack. 'We don't say "retard", Rachael. It's not kind.'

'Rachael can say whatever she likes.' Jack grinned, clearly thinking his younger sister was bound to appreciate his support.

She made a face as if Santa Claus had given her a parcel with a fizzing fuse sticking out of it. 'Who asked your poxy opinion?' she asked. 'Creep.'

If you've ever seen a chicken with its head freshly sliced off, that was Jack – strutting and cursing while Craig did hysterical giggling that worried me. All I'd seen around him so far was white, a non-colour, the worst, suggesting a life that could spin in any direction. By contrast Rachael's was a deep blue, representing the strength the youngest girl in *this* family obviously needed.

For a couple of seconds Jack was lost in black. He was snarling at Craig for his 'moronic giggling' – although his eyes were shiny with tears, his fists clenched, not against his brother but against the humiliation of crying his not-so-hard heart out.

'Leave our Craig alone! You always pick on him when you can't cope,' snapped Vanessa – I'd got her as purple. What that signalled, though, was a mystery: I felt so dizzy I was becoming confused.

Then all four of them were going at each other. Their voices had squeaky bits and gruff bits and God knew how many other bits wildly overlapping.

Ginger let out three or four sighs – the build-up to an explosion: 'If you bloody kids are going to turn this into yet another row, we're going home empty-handed – so you'd better stop right now!'

I was at my dizziest yet. As you are, when your only hope of survival is being nuked by the very family that's just stolen your heart.

4

The kids were on tenterhooks.

When Jack broke the awkward silence, I heard a tremor in his voice: he was trying to hold back the tears that were still in his eyes. 'We're sorry.' He really meant it. 'Aren't we?' he asked Vanessa.

She sidled close to him and gave his ribs an affectionate prod. 'Yes,' she agreed, her green peepers on her mum, whose right eyebrow arched so high it only needed a dot under it to become a question mark. 'You lot better start behaving,' she cautioned, prompting sighs of relief from Jack and Vanessa that made me want to bite the bars of my cage and rip them away – I was desperate to be part of the topsy-turvy love I could see right before my eyes.

But those kids scrapped like deranged alley cats – they couldn't have maintained a truce if their own lives had depended on it, let alone mine. Instead of keeping schtum, Rachael put her hands on her hips and exclaimed, 'Well, I didn't say a blinking word!'

Which was an invitation for Craig to retort, 'You called me a retard!' – with Jack adding, 'And me a creep!'

Well, no matter how much his little sister – who was

beady-eyed with fury – wanted to respond to that, she resisted: her mum had emitted an almighty groan.

There was another silence in which, once more, I feared for my life – until Vanessa came to the rescue. 'Mum, we absolutely *totally* promise not to argue any more,' she declared, looking daggers at her sister, who was still on the edge of snapping back at Jack. Instead she gave a shrug, which meant that, for the time being, she was biting her tongue.

'You too, Craig,' warned Vanessa. Her brow lifted in response to his salute, while Ginger smiled.

'Whatever you say, our Vee,' Jack concurred. 'So,' he then decreed, 'no more arguing.' He didn't look at Rachael and Craig in case he sparked another row, but now Vanessa wasn't the only one steering them – and me – away from the rocks. The mutts in the cages on the other side of the grass must have seen who was really in charge.

It would all of have been quite amusing if I hadn't been consumed by the burning hope that they'd get me away from Psycho Vet before Ginger did a complete Armageddon job.

But things seemed better: as though, despite her earlier stand-off with Jackie, Vanessa had become the ultimate peace broker. 'That's settled, then,' she announced, and offered Ginger a wry smile. 'We're truly sorry, Mum. We can't help ourselves. We're barbarians.'

At this point I was driven to call upon another feisty female spirit for help. 'If you're there, Your Hoityness, make it happen,' I prayed. 'Please.' I'd remembered that, for all her angry ways, I'd wanted Her Hoityness as a mum, her lovely black and yellow fur mine to snuggle into. Because, let's face it, at one human year old I was still pretty much a kid myself.

5

Craig was next to crouch before me, and right away I saw loss and pain behind his eyes. It reminded me of the pup that was told he should have been drowned to spare the world its repulsive self. Perhaps now one loser would reject another: the kid and me, worthless and vile, the pair of us.

But he broke into a huge grin and declared that I was a beautiful boy. Before I knew it, my tongue was between the horrid steel bars and licking his nose, which made him laugh and me feel better.

'A lovely beautiful darling,' he said, in Ginger's fetching OTT style.

Jack and Vanessa good-naturedly rolled their eyes to Heaven.

By now the kennel lad – who had thick blond hair and healthily tanned skin that I was *so* glad I hadn't bitten – had turned up.

'Blimey, our Craig!' exclaimed Rachael, as Ginger gave the newcomer a thumbs-up that set my heart pounding. 'You can't go around calling dogs lovely beautiful darlings! *Lovely beautiful darling!*' she mimicked, not unkindly. I actually barked with joy, causing her to laugh with everybody else, while Craig nodded, blushing, at the kennel lad, who winked at him and stepped back. He didn't want to intrude on the family that – would you believe? – now resumed its competitive ways.

'Craig can say "lovely beautiful darling" if he likes.' Jack smiled down at me and prodded his brother's shoulder with the toe of his shoe, as he'd done to my paw a few minutes earlier. 'Can't you, our kid?'

'Yup,' agreed Craig, who – concentrating on me – had stopped blushing. He glanced at the kennel lad for approval as he reached into my cage to feel my sore and wasted flanks. His eyes brightened, as if he'd hit on the answer to something dead important, like world hunger. 'And I'll tell youse what,' he announced. 'We'll call him Bruce!'

Well, there was a moniker! It wasn't daft like Biggles – and my seal wiggle was going so hard I could have been 90 per cent Labrador. My excitement grew when Jack declared that Bruce was a great name. 'In fact, I'd go so far as to say *bloody* great.' He crouched down again and slung his arm across Craig's shoulders. With them being so close, and so alike, and so happy, I was licking both their faces now, my poor nose getting knocked to bits on the steel bars as I shifted from one to the other.

'Look at them, Mum! Three crazy dogs!' exclaimed Vanessa.

'I think', said Ginger, to the grinning kennel lad, 'that Bruce has found his new home.'

But then she went and asked Rachael what she thought, causing another twist in the roller-coaster ride that had started when I'd noticed somebody lurking outside my cage.

'Not Bruce, *Blue*,' Rachael insisted, as she replaced Jack beside Craig on the concrete path – none of them would have got down on it if they'd seen what the kennel lad swilled off it.

Craig gritted his teeth, kept his eyes firmly on me and repeated, '*Bruce*,' until Vanessa decided that though 'Blue' was right for my eyes, she preferred Bruce too.

'Come on, Rach!' Jack urged. 'Be a good sport. Let Craig choose his name.'

The kennel lad suggested they put it to the vote. The kids' eyes were as wide as gobstoppers, their furry-caterpillar eyebrows so far up their foreheads that they were lost in their floppy black hair. Four fantastically quizzical express-ions that had Ginger laughing like a drain, probably because voting was a novelty in this family: usually whoever shouted loudest was the winner. 'I say!' She beamed at the kennel lad, whose well-proportioned features were en-hanced by the amusement in his pale blue eyes. 'What a simply fabulous idea! Why don't we do exactly that?'

'Because I'll lose,' Rachael shot back, and joined in with the hilarity that followed. 'Okay, our Craig,' she conceded. 'Bruce it is. But he'll get called Brucie anyway,' she added, as she got up from the concrete and joined Jack, Vanessa and Ginger.

Now they and the kennel lad waited for Craig's response to his sister's last remark.

He was unfazed by it. Once more his eyes lit up as if he'd

hit on the answer to another world problem – the halting of the arms race, perhaps. He kept his cheeky gaze on me as he said, 'Brucie-Wucie-Lucie darling!'

Everyone fell about laughing with sheer joy at my rebirth as Brucie. My first human had called me Runt.

'Brucie-Wucie-Lucie darling,' Craig repeated quietly, with a shy grin for the kennel lad, who said I was a fantastic dog. (I regretted all the more the time I'd wanted to bite him because he was answerable to Psycho Vet.)

'You'll love him to bits,' he added.

Craig turned crimson again. 'We love him already, thanks. Loads and loads,' he added, as he got up and went to stand with Vanessa and Jack. They were smiling between themselves, Ginger was thoughtful, and Rachael was as inscrutable as granite.

'Well,' said the kennel lad, at last slipping the bolt on my door. 'Brucie's all yours, folks.' With that he left me with my new family. And I discovered, to my delight, that I wasn't the only one who had fallen headlong that day. Now it was confirmed that, far from being worthless, I was a mutt who was adored like he never would have believed possible. I said a prayer of thanks to Her Hoityness.

6

Ginger signed my release forms while the kids took me outside to where a bumpy gravel car park overlooked a Sunday cricket pitch that was brown after weeks of sun and the hosepipe ban. We passed a gleaming yellow and chrome Raleigh Chopper chained to a post.

'That's his bike,' said Rachael, with interest. 'The kennel lad's.'

'So? What's the big deal?' asked Vanessa. Craig's grip tightened on my lead.

'None,' broke in Jack. 'Except that he was in our Craig's class.'

'And . . .' persisted Rachael, '. . . got taken away from school because he tried to do himself in.'

Vanessa told her that if the kennel lad had taken his mum's sleeping pills, like everybody said, then it was one thing Craig couldn't be blamed for. I wondered just how wonky my colour sense had gone: all I'd got from the kennel lad had been a promising red.

Still, I'd been getting an overload of colours. And something obviously *had* happened because Craig had been so awkward when the kennel lad appeared. I guessed this was because he'd been worried his ex-classmate would

18

think they'd all start talking about him. That, of course, was exactly what they'd just done, though this was one topic that even Rachael was glad to drop.

'Is Brucie okay?' called Ginger, as she came towards us.

The tension on my lead slackened.

'Mum, he's more than okay!'

'He's brilliant!' Jack punched the air.

7

The 'taxi' waiting on the far side of car park was a silver mini-bus with more dents than a tank that had taken a direct hit. 'Blimey,' said the driver, on seeing me. 'They must be low on dogs.' When he saw the kids' glares directed at him, he apologized hastily.

'Back to Shangri-La,' instructed Ginger, with a chuckle.

Maybe they lived in a semi with lace curtains and a lawn mown to resemble a carpet. Or not: I reckoned the family lacked a dad to cut the grass – or he'd have got a mention at least when it came to choosing a mutt.

'What's this Shangri-La place, then?' asked the driver, after he'd managed the tricky turn out of the car park and on to the road to the coast.

'Utopia!' chorused the kids.

Ginger laughed. Then she patted her thighs, inviting me to come to her. I stood up and put my front paws on her lap. 'Artful bugger,' she murmured, cupping my head in her hands and looking me in the eye as the dented silver mini-bus carried us towards my new home.

8

G inger was in a huff. 'Don't be so damn cheeky!'
  Rachael retorted, 'I was not!'
  Jack insisted, 'Oh yes you were!'

'You said Brucie'll think Mum's painted the front door like a boiled sweet!'

'Actually,' corrected Vanessa, 'she said Liquorice Allsort.'

'Who the heck cares?' Craig was tickling me between my ears where the hair was patchy, but not as bad as it was on my scabby back. 'If he can't cope with his first impression he'll be so freaked by the rest of the house he'll run back to the kennels. At top bloody speed!' he added. Everyone eyed him and me with tons of affection: like we already had a special bond. And I guessed we had. I loved all the kids but Craig was the one I felt most protective towards – the way some humans instinctively right a beetle that's on its back kicking helplessly at the air. But why this one kid in particular out of the four, I had no idea – as you might expect when I'd just tumbled out of the taxi in front of my new home. It was an old terraced house with a wide double-storey bay window and a peaked attic.

The first thing to get my attention was the sea, a hundred yards down the hill, a blue expanse so shimmery and *huge*, after my near-fatal confinement at the kennels, that I let out a big bark.

Jack thought I was objecting to a white marble statue of a little round human that looked over the waves from a paved promontory where steps led to the beach: 'Ha! Brucie doesn't care for Winston Churchill either!' he exclaimed, laughing at his mum.

Her response was swift but controlled, as if this Winston thing was part of an on-going battle of wits. 'If I've said it once, Jack, I've said it a thousand times. I have *nothing* against Winston Churchill. I merely resent the damn council sticking him there so that we no longer get a full sea view,' she said.

I reckoned the statue must be a recent addition: the previous year, 1975 – that of my birth – had marked the thirtieth anniversary of the war's end. I was starting to realize that, despite the time that had passed, the war was still meshed with Ginger's world – but now wasn't the time to think about that. Not least because Vanessa, Rachael and Craig were giving Jack looks to kill – by goading Ginger into an argument, he was spoiling my arrival for them all.

'Sorry, gang,' he said, shrugging his nice square shoulders. 'Only joking,' he added, to Ginger. She replied that she'd only-joke him if he didn't stop talking about things he couldn't begin to understand. That had him narked enough to retaliate and start a row that would have really done my dizzy head in – but before he could release the anger that had put blackness all around him again, I gathered what strength I had to leap Ginger's rusty garden gate. My entire body arched and swished through the air, making me feel so proud of myself that I wouldn't have swapped the life I was entering for all the luxury the Queen's Corgis enjoyed. (To be fair, they're less spoilt than many humans claim.)

'Wow!' Jack was impressed, as were my other kids and Ginger, but my mind had been grabbed by something else.

Just as Rachael had predicted, I *was* stunned by Ginger's front door: it had a black background with chunky blue-grey mouldings framing four bright pink rectangular panels. A horizontal brass letterbox created a smile of sorts: this was a *welcoming* door. Far from making me want to run back to the kennels, I felt at home. Especially when I took in the neighbour's perfect patch of grass. It would have alarmed me no end had it been Ginger's, because I'd have known I'd misread her – and totally misunderstood the kids. They were now lined up at the wall, watching me. I'd landed on the path beside a tiny square garden packed with irises that were yellow, pale blue and deep purple: a sweet-scented display that matched the vividness of the unusual Liquorice Allsort entrance to the house.

I was getting a feel for Ginger's love of growing things: whatever she nurtured exuded good health, not least the kids, who all had lovely smooth skin with a hint of olive.

'You see . . .' Vanessa was whispering, to avoid disturbing me, '. . . Rachael was right. He *was* taken aback by the door. And . . .'

'Now he's weighing up the garden,' murmured Jack.

'Because he's clever,' declared Rachael, proud that she

had accurately predicted my first response to our home. 'Dead clever.'

'Yeah,' agreed Craig, beaming as if I was a Crufts winner, not a scabby mutt, whose ears were pricked in total amazement at how his luck had changed.

Then, as if she was well and truly satisfied with how things were progressing, Ginger was all life again: opening the squeaky gate and sweeping by me to where the key was under a brick near the bay window. 'Okay, you bloody barmy lot,' she said.

'Leave Brucie to settle in. Otherwise', she declared, setting her shoulder to the Liquorice Allsort, which was stiff where it caught the frame, 'he'll end up as mad as the rest of us . . . Oh, blast!' The kids giggled as she tumbled into the porch. (She recovered her balance so quickly that I realized she often fell into her home.)

Under Ginger's watchful but welcoming eye, I passed through the Liquorice Allsort and a glass inner door into a passage that split into two: the stairs went straight up on the left, and to the right the passage ended at another door with oblong glass panes. It led into a kitchen where I glimpsed a grey parrot in a domed cage, which sent shivers through me: hard on my stay at the kennels, I'd hated all cages.

'Now he's got his eye on our Picasso,' observed Vanessa.

'Never mind that,' said Ginger, before anybody else could speak. 'Each of you is to get on with your own thing and leave Brucie to settle in. I'll make sure he doesn't eat the parrot,' she added, which annoyed me: I'd never harmed a fly in my life. Then she gave me a long, warm look.

'Actually, I couldn't imagine this animal hurting anything,' she said, and I was happy again.

Vanessa went to the front room where the bay window looked on to the irises, Rachael to the back room, Jack upstairs and – shooting a look over his shoulder as he passed though the kitchen – Craig wandered out of the back door. It struck me that he probably fiddled with bicycles – his hands were oil-stained.

When they'd gone, Ginger took a moment to absorb the silence, then looked at me wearily. Suddenly her eyes seemed less green and much smaller. 'Help me with them, Brucie,' she whispered, sealing my love for her. 'Please, help me with them.'

Ginger gave me some water in a glass mixing bowl which, until it got smashed after about five years, became known as Brucie's fish bowl. And while she busied herself in the kitchen, I lay at the foot of the stairs: an extra-snug place because the bottom step had a carpeted front that supported my side.

There I was, not ten minutes through the Liquorice Allsort, already resting with my chin between my paws in a home that – for the moment – was as quiet as a spinster's.

The door with the clear oblong panes through which I'd glimpsed Picasso opened so fast that the hard round Bakelite handle hit the wall. The plaster crumbled. The thwack gave me such a shock that I jumped up – straight into the path of Ginger, who was tearing up the corridor quicker than a Whippet.

'Out of the way, damn dog!' she spluttered. 'Which of you wretched kids has *stolen* my handbag?' she yelled, so loud that her words likely reached the marble lugs of Sir Winston Churchill. Who, if he'd still had his wits about him, would have dived off his promontory into the sea, thereby escaping a probable attack on his person.

have said more if Jack and Vanessa hadn't noticed the unhappiness that was clouding their mum's beautiful battered face.

'Enough, Craig,' they said as one.

Ginger was emphatic. Her purse had been in her pocket when she had gone to the kennels, so her handbag, which she needed because she had to go to the bank, must be somewhere in the house.

'I'll do downstairs, Mum,' sighed Rachael.

'And I'll do upstairs,' said Vanessa. 'You do the attics, Craig.'

'And I'll do the oven, shall I?' suggested Jack. At first I thought he was being sarky, but then saw he was teasing his mum out of her misery. It was a ploy Vanessa understood – she looked away to hide a smile.

'Just look sharp, the lot of you!' ordered Ginger. 'Find my damn handbag! And no shirking! Do you hear me? *No* shirking!'

Off they went, soon forgetting their allotted search areas as every cushion, pillow, bedspread and all else was turned. They criss-crossed each other on all three floors of the house while becoming more and more annoyed, until really it didn't matter who was saying what to whom. The lingo went more or less like this: 'Have you seen it?'

'Get lost, you're not even looking.'

'Don't look at me. I didn't put it anywhere.'

'Well, I haven't seen it.'

'Since when have you ever found it anyway?'

'Up yours.'

'Up yours too.'

'Do you two have to be so downright vulgar?'

'Piss off.'

'Aye, piss off, Goody Two Shoes.'

'Oh, run and jump, the lot of you!'

All of which played out against Ginger's cries of: 'Find my handbag! Will you indolent young people please be bothered to find my handbag?'

If you're thinking that maybe I took my chance to have a good squint at the place, I was so dizzy with following the kids up and down stairs that I'd hardly taken in anything beyond a strong impression of a rambling Victorian house that would have given the horrors to anybody inclined to tidiness.

Then Jack went still and cocked his ear, like he was hearing the voice of God Almighty.

'What's with you?' asked Vanessa.

'No more shouting,' he replied. His sisters, brother and even I listened to a silence that had arrived like an unannounced guest.

'She's done it again!' declared Vanessa.

'She's always doing it!' thundered Craig.

'The bay window!' called Rachael, already descending the stairs two at a time. She led us to the big front room where there was a framed wartime photograph of young Ginger – with an unbroken nose – and a bearded sailor with thick black hair and eyebrows, which meant he was unquestionably the kids' dad. I like to think he would have laughed if he'd seen the indignant faces of my little pack as they grouped in the window and watched Ginger go out through the garden gate with her handbag tucked under her arm, a big grin on her face as she avoided looking at them.

'She found it wherever she put it so she wouldn't flaming lose it!' exclaimed Rachael.

'She's a pain in the bum,' muttered Craigie, as his mother crossed the wide road, which was covered in tarmac dyed red with spoil from old coal mines up the coast.

'She's worse than that,' concluded Jack, on tiptoe to peer after her as she strode up the hill to the town centre. 'She's so far round the bloody bend she's meeting herself coming back!'

'Actually,' corrected Vanessa, allowing a moment to pass before she made the point that explained why they had only one parent, 'she's grieving for Daddy.'

As she watched her mum going up the road with her handbag under her arm, Rachael took hold of one of the long gold velvet curtains – even when they were open, they still covered part of the glass and she wanted the best view she could get. Now she let go and stepped back into the room. 'We agreed not to talk about Raymond.'

From the way she said the name, I knew she was issuing a challenge. I was proved right when Vanessa reddened and snapped, 'I've told you before, Rachael – he isn't Raymond, he's Daddy.'

'To you, maybe,' retorted Rachael, who didn't yet have tears in her eyes like her older sister, 'but to me he's a bad memory that hangs about like a horrible smell. And', she went on, 'he wasn't exactly kind to our Craig either. Was he?' she demanded of her twin, whose eyes, at the mention of his dad, had lost their sparkle.

'He wasn't that bad,' he replied, sounding hollow.

'He was a pig,' spat Rachael, the force of her words crinkling her furry caterpillars. 'A pig who knocked Mum about.' She scowled at her sister, daring her to question this fact – which Vanessa had a go at doing.

'Only when he'd been drinking,' she said.

'It's too hard to call Dad a pig,' Jack put in. 'He was a screw-up. A total screw-up who couldn't help himself.'

'Because of all the terrible things in his head,' Vanessa added, almost pleading for mercy with the memory of the bearded man in the photograph with young Ginger.

'He still knocked Mum about,' insisted Rachael. 'He punched her. He kicked her. He dragged her upstairs by the hair.'

Well, that had Craig and Vanessa staring at the floor, and Jack moving so close to Rachael that I feared he was going to lash out. 'For Christ's sake, you little madam, we know all that stuff,' he said angrily. 'And now you've reminded us so graphically of his many sins', he continued, looking pretty scary from where I was, 'you'll be pleased to recall that he died quite horribly, won't you?'

'He didn't *die*, like normal people!' Rachael retorted. 'He put himself in the sea, remember? That's not dying, our Jack. That's suicide. The coward's way out!'

Imagine a mighty oak that's had a power-saw through its trunk but hasn't toppled: for a few moments, that was Jack.

Then, as his eyes filled with tears, he said, 'Put bluntly as that, Rachael, you're right. If being violent makes somebody a pig, then a pig Dad was.' I could feel his pain. 'But Mum was the one he knocked about,' he went on. 'So if it's okay for her to love him, we shouldn't feel guilty about it.'

Vanessa stepped close to Rachael, who'd now got wet eyes like everybody else. 'He isn't *Raymond*, Rachael,' she said, but not harshly. 'He's our father.'

'Was,' retorted her sister, eyeballing her.

12

So there they were. Stuck with nothing else to say. At least until Craig launched himself against the big old sofa, grabbed Jack's neck, brought him down, then sat on his belly and pinned his arms to the floor. 'Get out of that!' he exclaimed, throwing a gleeful glance at his sisters. The upturned sofa had made a loud crack, followed by a heavy thump. I'd half expected the floorboards to be damaged because Ginger had an old-fashioned centre rug, not a fitted carpet.

'You two maniacs better not have broken another sofa!' warned Vanessa.

'Mum'll go ape if you have!' cried Rachael 'It'll be the third in six months – no wonder we get furniture Steptoe and Son would reject.'

'Actually,' said Jack, who was breathless and giggling between the sofa and the wall, 'it's only the second. Bastard!' he added – Craig was fighting hard to keep him pinned down as he twisted to free himself. 'Sir Wankalot here attacked when I didn't expect it,' he spluttered, his eyes bulging like a Pug's as he gave the kid a pretend-angry look.

'Of course he did, our Jack,' teased Vanessa.

'Tell another porky and we might believe it!' cried Rachael.

Jack worked his arms free, and Craig, swinging his own limbs away from his brother's suddenly searching hands, hit the thin aluminium frame on the biggest of Ginger's paintings, which hung throughout the house.

'Mind what you're doing!' yelled Rachael. I stared at the colourful image of a Mississippi riverboat that sailed mid-stream, grey smoke chuffing from a pair of thin black chimneys topped with spikes, like the teeth of the Devil.

'Spoil that and you're both *dead!*' promised Vanessa, moving back as Jack and Craig reared up from the floor: a writhing double-headed beast that fell against the upturned sofa, which – with another loud crack – was righted by their weight. I was wiggling like a whole pod of seals as Vanessa and Rachael completed the family lunacy by screaming at them for being idiots.

Idiots who were fast standing up: they had tumbled off the sofa on to the dark blue tiled hearth where the poker, tongs, coal shovel and accompanying brush got scattered with a racket that gave me the jitters – though this was nothing compared to what followed.

As they finally untangled, my *very* giggly kids staggered like drunkards and Jack accidentally brushed against some of the many knick-knacks atop the grey marble mantel. There was a smash, and a moment of utter quiet before he and Craig dared to look at the framed photograph of Ginger and Raymond, now face down on the hearth, its glass shattered by the poker handle.

'Oh, shit!' they cried.

'Idiots!' repeated Vanessa and Rachael.

13

The photograph was of the kids' parents as child-hood sweethearts. They had got divorced after the war, then remarried years later when a doctor had advised that Raymond – who had been sober for nearly a decade – was finally over his war trauma. A second set of twins had fast followed the first.

'We didn't mean to break it,' protested Craig, alarmed, as Rachael carefully removed the few pointy shards that had stayed in the frame, their razor sharp edges slashing over the faces of young Raymond and Ginger.

Jack had quickly rallied after the accident and told him not to panic. All that was needed was new glass.

'I suppose you're going to pay for it?' asked Rachael, as she put the glassless but otherwise unharmed photograph back on the mantel.

Her question had him scratching his unruly hair as if he'd got nits.

'If we must,' he replied, with a sigh that was directed at Vanessa, who'd been wearing a faraway look.

Her sudden declaration 'Nobody has to pay!' proved she'd been thinking about the problem.

'How so?' asked her twin.

'Because, dear dummies,' Vanessa explained, 'I have a framed school photo the same size. So', she smiled, 'all we have to do is swap the glass.'

'Good,' responded Rachael, as she headed out of the room to bin the broken glass.

'Excellent!' declared Jack, and got on with the nit-scratching routine.

'Brilliant!' Craig was so relieved he bowed his head; Vanessa dropped a self-mocking curtsy.

'Well done, Vanessa,' called Rachael, out of sight now.

'Yeah, well done, Vee,' Jack quietly agreed, as he followed Craig's gaze to where young Ginger and Raymond faced into the room.

'Don't they look strange . . .' Craig frowned, '. . . without the glass? They look . . .'

'Vulnerable?' suggested his elder sister. It was the exact word he was perhaps too young to find. For some reason it made me shiver again.

14

The photograph was quickly repaired, and I had a proper dizzy turn – it was almost as bad as when my first human had used his special cable: the one with a three-pin plug, for connecting to the mains, and the exposed wires for touching to my back. It lost more hair each time he punished me. But with the new dizziness, I went into a black space from which I heard Craig's voice, so distressed. I felt sad like never before – except when I'd realized why my first human was so cruel: it was as if, even on the brightest day, he was stuck somewhere fearsome all by himself.

Then I worried that he'd attach the special cable to his own private parts. His on–off girlfriend had found him like that one night when he was drunk and self-loathing, as if, in his own eyes he was the ugliest human ever. The twist was that this might have been true. Because afterwards – when he was back to hating others more than himself – he'd head-butted her for what he called her effing interference in coaxing him not to flick the switch that would have zapped him.

Anyway, Craig's distress at my collapse felt as though he was tugging at a lead attached to my collar. 'Brucie's dying!'

he cried, unaware that his panic was bringing me round to soothe him: taking care of the kids was already my sole purpose for living. 'He's dying! He's dying!' He flapped so hard that as soon as my vision returned I licked his hand. It had the sickly taste of terror. My fear of the black that had nearly taken me was washed away by the sight of them crouched close and peering at me with eyes of love. Many humans would have blatted my head on the pretext of ending my misery.

'He's not dying, ya daft bugger, Craig!' exclaimed Rachael, who always led on medical matters – she had her Duke of Edinburgh Award first-aid certificate. 'He's had a fit,' she explained, cradling the side of my head in her palm. She diagnosed that, despite the water Ginger had given me, I was dehydrated.

'That makes sense,' agreed Vanessa, who sounded every bit as relieved as Craig was suddenly looking. 'That and overexcitement,' she added, rebuking her brothers for half wrecking the place when I was meant to be calmly settling in, as their mum had ordered.

Jack looked as guilty as a robber and kissed my ear (doubtless he saw it as the bit least likely to give him scabs). 'Sorry, Brucie,' he said, shooting a glance at Craig, who now looked so troubled you would have thought he'd deliberately tried to off me by starting the fun-fight with Jack.

'Oh, come off it!' said Rachael. 'We were all mucking about. We can't blame our Craig. Or you for that matter, Jack – *unfortunately*! It was all of us. And that's that.'

The blue around her was like an evening sky in summer

and every heart in the room was touched by how she'd boosted her twin. Craig, in fearing my own sudden death, had expressed their mutual grief at the loss of their father.

Vanessa filled my fish bowl to the brim. I lapped so fast that Jack reckoned I must have been dehydrated to the point of dust. While his sisters smiled at that, Craig was suddenly very thoughtful. At last a question that had long been inside him now forced its way out – like Her Hoityness, who'd once birthed a stillborn nobody knew she was carrying. It was the result of an encounter with a Dalmatian, on a runaway trip along the beach to where a lighthouse stood on rocks called the Island: one highly inconvenient tiny white surprise, right at the feet of her humans (who were watching *Coronation Street*). The pup was there for all to witness, no pretending otherwise, like the kid's unexpected question: 'But why did Mum not hate Dad?'

'C'mon, you lot,' he demanded, defying the silence of Rachael, Vanessa and Jack. 'I know youse can answer. Why did Mum never hate Dad? Especially', he added, with a not unkind look at Rachael, 'when he did stuff like drag her upstairs by the hair.'

'Because', sighed Jack, 'they fell in love before the war wrecked his head.'

'Precisely,' agreed Vanessa, who was now also addressing

her doubtful-looking sister. 'They fell in love before he was damaged. And if you take that away', she insisted, as Rachael made to protest, 'then you lose the beauty. The fact that, despite the bad stuff, they once loved each other.'

Vanessa seemed taken aback by how far she'd gone, while the two brothers shared a look of amazement to rival that of Her Hoityness's humans upon seeing the dead puppy on their fireside rug (which, apparently, was Persian, and highly prized).

'Well . . .' mused Rachael, '. . . if being dragged upstairs by the hair while your screaming kids see your bloomers is beauty, remind me never to fall in love.'

To which even Vanessa – whose right eyebrow became the same question mark as Ginger's had been earlier that day – had nothing to say.

16

The kids came out of their pensive mood. They forced the wrecked sofa – which had reclined, like a deckchair – back into shape. Then, with lots of giggling, they agreed that, when Ginger was settled on her comfy chair to the right of the fireplace, they would sit together on the sofa: its back would 'break' under their combined weight. Their fun was all the greater because they knew their mum would understand what was going on, but would be unable to prove it.

Now, with cuddles from Rachael, Jack and Craig – who whispered in my ear, 'Don't die on us, Brucie darling' – I was left in the front room with Vanessa, who'd got a load of blue material and sewing stuff. She'd been preparing to do some dressmaking when Ginger had started yelling about her handbag.

Anyway, after she'd tested her own weight on the dodgy sofa, she patted for me to climb up beside her and started cutting the blue material into strips. Ginger's velvet curtains hung temptingly at the bay window. 'Velvet is *nice*, isn't it, Brucie?' she said, absently tickling between my ears. She was staring at the shiny gold material, like a boozer wanting somebody else's glass of whisky. 'And gold's such a good colour,' she added.

Clearly she considered that velvet was hers for the taking.

My point was proved moments later when she was standing on a little cabinet she'd brought over from a corner. Her face twisted with the effort of releasing the brass screw that kept the curtain hooks from slipping off the metal rail, her body silhouetted against the glass. I noticed her blue jeans were turned up with yellow inch-long stitches as higgledy-piggledy as a happy drunk's thinking. The zany imperfection of that stitching had my heart swelling with love: it was as if I already knew Vanessa would always do her own colourful thing. Including nicking her mum's long gold velvet curtain. Its hooks had tiny steel wheels that slid from the rail with a squeaky whoosh.

'There,' she declared, as she resettled herself beside me, with a guilty glance at the fully exposed panes to the seaward side of the bay. 'She'll never notice.' Killing the uncertainty that had entered her voice, she repeated, 'Never,' and scissored the curtain before she could change her mind. She would have faced a hundred deaths before she gave up on anything she had set her heart on.

17

All dogs know this: you never use your second sight unless you've got all your strength. But with everything I'd seen and felt, I was determined that, by the end of my first day at Ginger's, I'd understand each of the kids, starting with Vanessa. She had already cut a wide strip from the bottom of the curtain: a strip that I rightly guessed was for making a skirt with the higgledy-piggledy sewing I'd seen on her turned-up jeans – except that, from the colour of the bob of cotton she'd got waiting on the arm of the sofa, I knew the stitches would be purple, not yellow. That had me laughing inside: with her choice of gold and purple my young human had a regal turn of mind (maybe I should have been a Corgi, after all).

I emitted a happy groan. Vanessa paused in her work to look at me questioningly. I thought she was going to speak, but she just gave me a smile that made me snuggle closer to the gold velvet that was rumpled on her lap like a big rose. I took a deep breath that filled my lungs with her sweetness, then surrendered to sleep. And to whatever my second sight would reveal about her.

18

The black that came this time reminded me of how it must have been before I was born into my cruel early life: warm and protected, with no worries. Then I got a taste of salt and heard lapping waves. My second sight opened to a large, curved and shiny steel needle that was being worked through pre-pressed holes on the leather moccasin Raymond was stitching. His fingers were brown where he held his cigarettes, and black from fixing cars (I'll come to that later).

Vanessa was sitting next to him on the edge of the rocks with her bare feet dangling in the sea, which was throwing off millions of sunny sparkles. He smiled. 'So, you want to know why your old dad's making a pair of slippers?'

'That's right,' she replied, affectionately cheeky. Whatever his faults, his daughter's love made it clear that Raymond wasn't so easily written off as a bad human (that would have made my understanding of things much easier). 'I mean, why moccasins?' she continued.

'Why not?' teased Raymond. He'd got alcohol oozing out of every pore, but he seemed content. 'And besides,' he went on, splashing with his feet, 'what's up with moccasins?

They're still slippers, our Vee.' He chuckled when she told him she'd never claimed they weren't.

His feet were still in the water as he squinted to see far ahead. The whites of his eyes were yellowy; if he hadn't been an alky, I'd have said he had conjunctivitis: the same problem as me. Using her hands to shield her eyes, Vanessa followed the direction of his gaze. 'Well, Dad? *Are* they still in the same place, or not?'

He replied that they were. I, too, peered at where a grey ship on the horizon was towing a rusty wreck: to the breakers, I guessed, until something that resembled a scaffolding bar came flying from the lead vessel towards the water. It landed with a bang and a splash that carried to us. Vanessa winced as if this distant shell practice was aimed at her dad's heart. She looked at him. He was now so still that I got the feeling he daren't move in case he went to pieces. Gently she advised him to finish his sewing. 'After all,' she explained, as if she was entering mined waters, 'it's less upsetting than guns at sea.'

'Ah' replied Raymond. 'That's something you know nothing about, darling. Nothing at all. And . . .' he said, as he lowered his eyes to the half-made moccasin, '. . . hopefully, you never will.'

She responded with a lack of drama that made me wish I was actually there and could nuzzle her; I was so proud of her care for Raymond, whose shaggy fag-stained beard was as grey as his eyebrows and unkempt hair. 'We all love you, Dad – me, Jack, Rachael, and Craig. Whatever you think, we all love you.'

At that, his lips quivered, as if he was crying inside. 'I'm not sure I'm lovable, our Vanessa,' he explained, working the curved needle through the next hole in the sable-coloured leather. 'Not for some time,' he added, careful not to look, her green eyes being so full of tears that they reflected sparkles of the sea. She didn't actually cry, though.

'Mum loves you too. Mum loves you loads. In fact, Mum just wants you to stop drinking.' She sounded as though she'd just made a panicky swim for dear life. This time when a shell on the horizon went off, she flinched for herself, not for Raymond, who paused with his needle halfway through the layers he was joining together.

'Maybe', he said, turning a steady eye on her, 'your mother would be wise to give up on me.'

That statement was taking them somewhere lonely and horrible so she played a Ginger-style game of anger, snapping, 'Then where would you be, you daft man? Honestly, Dad, you do my head in! You really do! No wonder Mum nags you.'

'No wonder,' he agreed, aware like her that now there was nowhere safe for their talk to go.

'Whatever . . .' shrugged Vanessa, then reminded him that he still hadn't told her *why* he was making moccasins.

'For my feet,' he responded, smiling to himself as he continued sewing.

19

I was back to a darkness so calming it was as if I was wrapped in velvet: now I knew that, however sad things had been for Vanessa, her dad hadn't vented his anger at her.

And into this comforting place came voices.

'Make me a promise, Daddy.'

'Depends what it is, Vee.'

'Give up drinking. For all of us. For the family. Give up drinking. Please?' she asked.

My darkness had lifted, and I was seeing them at the top of the beach steps beside Sir Winston; he was under a green tarpaulin, awaiting his civic unveiling.

'I'll make you a promise,' Raymond said, after a while, his eyes flitting above her head to where the sea's sparkles were being killed by a fast-approaching black cloud, 'and that promise', he continued, touching her chin with the side of his finger, 'is that I'll never again make my family a promise I can't keep.'

Vanessa's face was creasing with thought when the cloud was upon them with all the chaos you'd expect from millions of tiny bodies, with twice as many beating wings.

'Good God!' exclaimed Raymond, spitting one of the

creatures from his mouth as he got down low and clasped his daughter to him. 'Good God!' The air was now as black and dense as it was alive. 'Amazing! Extraordinary!' He released Vanessa but remained crouched as the swarm crossed the promenade, making for the sloped streets that led to the town centre. 'Ladybirds, Vanessa!' He laughed, his hands framing her face as he planted a kiss of reassurance on the middle of her forehead. Seeing him reborn by a freak of nature, she was joyful, too, her wide green eyes as beautiful to me as anything on earth.

'Ladybirds, Daddy!' She threw her arms out and her head back as she looked to where the statue stood beneath its green covering. 'Ladybirds, Sir Winston, you old bugger!' she sang.

'Ladybirds, Sir Winston, you old bugger!' they crooned crazily together, as Raymond led his daughter in a foot-stomping march around the promontory, an escapade that climaxed with a joint salute at where I knew Sir Winston's hard marble eyes faced out to sea.

'Ladybirds, Sir Winston, you old bugger!' they sang once more, unconcerned that people passing in cars were staring as if the strange-looking man and the girl with him were bonkers.

Raymond was sweaty and breathless and had flumped to a slatted bench at the feet of Sir Winston. His and Vanessa's laughter faded as she sat beside him. They looked out at the smooth sea, which had recovered its sparkles. Carefully, he told her to remember always that he'd loved his family the best he possibly could. My heart twisted with sorrow for him.

'Ships are going, Daddy,' she said, as she looked to where the shell practice had taken place on the horizon that the ladybirds had came from.

20

I spotted a red and yellow van motoring along the road behind them. In itself it wouldn't have been unusual, except that, to accompany the vivid white and pink ice cream painted on its side, a large plastic hot dog oozing tomato ketchup sat on its roof. All in all, it was a bizarre vehicle, which used to park near the home of my first human. The driver was known by everybody as Tony the Italian Number Two: he was the eldest son of Tony the Italian Number One who, everybody also knew, had been a prisoner of war and had married an English human when the fighting stopped.

It was a reminder of my former life that made me fear I would never really escape what had been done to me. Thankfully Vanessa grabbed my attention: she jumped up from the bench with her hand to her face, as if she'd got wind of a truly awful stink. 'Oh!' she cried. 'Oh!' She bent double, as if she was actually being gassed. 'Oh!' She pointed wildly at her nose.

Raymond glanced round, wondering who else could have broken wind. He discounted Sir Winston, of course.

'For God's sake, Daddy!' she squealed. 'It's not *that*! It's a horrible little thing right here!' She jabbed between her eyes with a finger that must have sounded like thunder to the ladybird in question – which, when you think, must have been the most surprised of them all. One moment she was in a fast-moving swarm, and the next she was up the nostril of a human with zero chance of getting out alive. At least, not according to Raymond's immediate remedy.

'Blow your nose!' he instructed, offering a grey but not exactly filthy hanky – just as his white open-neck shirt and blue slacks were grubby but not *dirty*-dirty. 'Blow hard!' he ordered.

I had visions of the ladybird getting blasted out of Vanessa's nose and crushed into the material – its punishment for going where it shouldn't have. Except that Raymond's simple plan was already useless because Vanessa's highly unwelcome guest was slipping further back. 'Get it out, Daddy!' she wailed. 'Get it out now! *Please!*' she begged – as if Raymond could have used the curved needle from his moccasin-making kit to extract the insect.

'Get it out!' she demanded, stamping her feet during the long moments it took her dad to devise plan B.

'Okay.' He returned the suspect hanky to his pocket, then instructed her to put her head back and keep still while he took a deep breath.

Raymond blew so hard up her nostrils that her face briefly resembled a half-inflated football. The expansion ended the second he removed his lips and followed her amazed stare as the ladybird flew out of her mouth, its wings flapping furiously. I caught myself thinking it was probably drunk because of Raymond's alky breath.

'Thank God for that!' wailed Vanessa, sinking back on to the bench below Sir Winston. 'That was *horrible*.' She shuddered. 'The most horrid thing ever!'

21

As for me, I was so taken aback by the ladybird stuff that, to begin with, I took no notice of Vanessa calling my name. And, besides, as far I could see, she wasn't saying it at all: she was still on the promontory, cuddling and thanking Raymond (who'd got a proud look that made me think he could have been a good dad all along). But then my second sight – or dream, if you prefer – gave way to where she was posing in the strip of gold velvet that was now a skirt with inch-long purple stitches.

'Stylish or what?' she asked, as my eyes readjusted to the room with the bay window.

To which – because I *always* encourage my kids – I made points of my ears and offered my most concentrated eyes: another trick that has humans adoring us.

'Twiggy, eat your heart out!' she exclaimed, posing like a model before she flopped back on the sofa and set about making a blouse and sash to match the skirt, an outfit that would go down in family history. Just like Raymond's moccasins.

* * *

As soon as Vanessa had recovered from having the ladybird up her nose, her dad went to get sloshed at the Gay Hussar where he left his moccasin-making kit. Thereby giving rise to the question that's still occasionally asked today: 'I wonder who's wearing Dad's slippers.'

22

Uplifted by my findings about Vanessa, I nosed my way to the back room where I discovered Rachael on a blue gym mat that took up most of the floor. Her stamina as she did one press-up after another was fantastic, but the thing that really delighted me was the healthy smell of her sweat. If the robustness of character I'd seen so far was nothing but a front, the scent as she pushed her body hard would have been acrid – I'd smelt that on Psycho Vet when the baking hot days made her neck and armpits wet. It was the reek of childhood misery that – despite the offing of Her Hoityness and Psycho's fatal intention for me – had saddened me.

My feelings for young Rachael couldn't have been more different. I trembled with delight as I noted she was wearing crimson tracksuit bottoms: red had replaced the blue that had earlier been her colour – proof that as well as being tough inside she was also good at sport. The tennis racquet, hockey stick, rounders bat and shuttlecocks in the white-painted room showed that her range was as wide as her determination was strong. Now she proudly did press-up number two hundred.

'Hello, Mr Big Dog!' she called. 'Watch me!' She began an

extra fifty press-ups, which got *faster* as I paced round the blue mat, so thrilled by her energy and muscular arms you would have thought I was her personal trainer.

All of which freed my second sight without the need for sleep: with Rachael still vigorously counting her exercises, I actually became her, reclining in a black vinyl dental chair and gazing into the piggy brown eyes of an elderly dentist with florid cheeks and a wig like a fireside rug.

Naturally enough, the voice that came out of my mouth was hers, complete with the resolve of Ginger delivering a nuclear blast – as I'd heard when she'd chided her squabbling kids.

'Absolutely not!' she said, into the face of the dentist with the rug on his head.

'Last week you said I needed two fillings. This week when I've come for those two fillings, you say I need four! You're a conman,' she added, taking off the plastic bib as she stood up. 'A Mr Nogood who bodges perfectly healthy teeth for money! You ought to be ashamed,' she concluded, giving the dentist – whose name was in fact Mr Nosgood – a glare before striding outside, where everything was covered with snow.

Snow that was fast gone when Rachael triumphantly reached her target: 'Two hundred and fifty!' She flopped down on the blue gym mat and rolled on to her back with her eyes closed and a satisfied smile on her lips (which, up close, were slightly thicker than the rest of the kids').

'Two hundred and fifty, Brucie,' she said, opening her eyes and carefully rubbing either side of my neck.

I stood looking down at her with my tail doing its gentlest wag. Not many kids would have had the nerve to challenge a bodging dentist from the very chair he'd trapped them in: that's what I understood as my tongue – it's always wanted to be involved in everything – licked her nose. Out of all the kids' snouts, it was most like young Ginger's in the wartime photograph with Raymond.

'Pooh, Brucie! Stinky breath!' She laughed and kissed my nose.

23

My investigations into the girls had gone so well that I was on a high when I found Jack in an upstairs room, working on a big oil painting set on an easel in the middle of the floor that – apart from an unmade divan and a tallboy with clothes bulging out of it – was largely taken up by canvases resting against each other, at least five deep to the walls. My discovery that the lad was a highly productive painter might have made me dizzy again, but his concentration was so intense that, if anything, he calmed me.

'Hello, Brucie,' he said, keeping his eyes on his work as I sniffed turps and oil. Every colour imaginable was smudged on the floorboards around his scruffy brogues. When he moved on to bigger things, that paint-stained area of Ginger's house would be just as much a record of his early period as his finished paintings. I got a good look at the picture on the easel then and had to block a yelp. It was of Elvis Presley. I knew all about him because my first human had gone mental each time it was reported that Elvis was in hospital. Jack's picture had shocked me because it captured the red, yellow, blue and gold sequins of the famous jumpsuits dissolving into sickly swirls of white, black and a liquidy pink, which I guessed was poor Elvis's fat. It was a devastating impression, in which the only precise detail was a blue eye with a yellowed white: an eye that – whether Jack knew it or not – was his dead father's, not Elvis Presley's. My love wasn't for the two destroyed humans on the canvas, though: it was for Jack, who was now using a thickly loaded palette knife to add a slash of crimson to the top right corner. As if the canvas bled.

'Lie down,' he said, as he glanced at me with eyes so intelligent I wondered if licking the back of his hand would increase my IQ. My first human had always said I was as stupid as I was worthless.

'Rest, Brucie, rest,' he added, as he got on with his work. Barely a minute passed before I entered my deepest sleep so far.

24

Raymond staggered into the path of two passing Salvation Army soldiers who were heading for the unveiling of Sir Winston's statue by the Mayor. 'My wife is going through my puppies!' he protested, as the man and woman hurried around him and down the road. 'Through my puppies,' he repeated sadly, as he threw a confused glance to the Liquorice Allsort and the glass inner door, which were open. Ginger was inside and out of sight. She was screeching that he was nothing but 'a lousy excuse for a man whose only friend is his next drink'.

Jack – who was watching his dad from where he was sitting on the garden wall – winced as if a knife had been slipped between his ribs. Raymond was so drunk he didn't care that he was in his birthday suit and outside the house. Now he caught his son's eye as if he was seizing a rock to resist the tide, staggering this way, then that, maintaining eye contact against all the odds. 'My wife,' he protested yet again.

'*Your damnable mother* is going through my puppies! Through my puppies!' he roared, straightening his back. Immediately he was off-balance, his dangly bit whipping aside as he did a dangerous double spin down the slope that ended when he slapped his hands on to the boot of a shiny gold car parked at the neighbour's house. An amazed – and even rather sweet – laugh escaped him when he realized he was unharmed. If his boozy ballet had brought him down, the sharp-edged black stone of the kerb could have been nasty – his face already bore the scars of previous tumbles.

'My wife, your *mother*', he emphasized, without looking at Jack, 'is going through my puppies.'

Now his anger was spent and his lips trembled within their bushy surround. His large head seemed even bigger than usual because the mass of his steely hair was ruffled. He tried to focus on the flecks in the metallic paint of the boot lid.

'Through my puppies.' He sobbed. His entire body, which was hairy and muscular save for a loose belly, crumpled in submission.

Jack jumped off the wall and walked over to him. 'Pockets not puppies, Dad,' he explained, adding kindly, as he led the way through the rusty garden gate, 'and she's only doing it because you've gone and spent the shopping money on a bender, ya daft old bugger.'

Which I suppose was where the immediate turmoil would have ended, except that before Raymond could take another step the downstairs window to the side of the bay was lifted so fast you heard the sash weights inside the frame clunk the wood.

'Get a move on, Jack!' hissed Vanessa, whose red face was as urgent as a boiling kettle. 'Craig says the bloody Salvation Army couple are telling a copper at the unveiling!'

Following the direction of her finger, her twin glanced up to where the kid had opened the upstairs sash, which had a clear view to the promontory, so hard that the weights broke away from the old cords. The clatter made Raymond giggle as if he was being tickled with feathers. 'Oops-a-daisy!' he teased, his bleary blue eyes widening at Craig, who was visibly alarmed at having damaged yet another bit of the house (as the kids were always doing). At this point, the unweighted window dropped on to Craig's neck. The kid now resembled the salami coming out of the side of a sandwich (but cold meat can't spew the lingo that had Vanessa craning out to see what was going on).

'Oops-a-daisy!' snickered Raymond, this time because he had lost his balance again, nearly tumbling into Ginger's colourful irises. Jack, distracted by Craig's accident, had let go of him.

Leastways, that was the situation until Rachael came up behind Craig and lifted the window off his neck. She stayed there, her arm raised in what seemed to be an ironic Nazi salute to Sir Winston as his green tarpaulin was removed, although she was in fact holding up the window against a second guillotining of her twin. Craig was busy examining his throat, making sure his Adam's apple hadn't been turned into an Adam's pear.

Next, she looked down to where Jack had got a firmer grip on Raymond and said, 'Let the flipping police arrest him.'

Which in turn had Vanessa calling up to her that everybody at school would see it in the papers.

Cottoning on to the possibility of handcuffs, Raymond

uttered a startled 'Eh?' that made Jack laugh as if he was the one who'd spent three days on the booze.

Rachael said she was only kidding, and could they please get a move on – not least because the copper in question was on the hundred-yard walk up the slope to find Raymond. Who, in case they had forgotten, was stark naked when it'd been in the news that the authorities were cracking down on streakers. Her outpouring caused her dad to applaud her debating skills. 'Well put, our Rachael,' he called proudly, smiling up at her as he advanced to the doorstep.

But Ginger blocked his path.

25

'Oh, no, you don't!' Ginger cried, a blob of her spit landing on Raymond's face. He was wearing a knocked-sideways expression – like what he really wanted was a good long sleep. 'You don't! You don't come into *this* house in *that* state! Pathetic sozzled spendthrift!' she added, and went on and on with more of the same, drowning Jack's pleas not to antagonize his dad, just this once.

Or, at least, that was how it was until she did the opposite of what her son wanted and stepped forward, driving Raymond backwards down the garden path. The three kids at the bay windows were begging them to quit because the copper was now halfway up the street.

'Worthless excuse for a man!' she spat.

Those words made me hopeful that she and Raymond played growls over serious violence – a notion that was blown to smithereens by the crunch of her nose under his fist.

'Bitch!' he snarled, eyes bulging, mouth and cheeks drawn murderously tight. I glimpsed a terrifyingly black and lonely soul. 'Vile, vile bitch!' he spewed, while Rachael, Craig and Vanessa pleaded with him to leave their mum alone. Raymond must have heeded them to some extent: he redirected his second punch away from her face, but it still met the side of her head. She reeled back to the open Liquorice Allsort as strange calm descended.

'Carry on,' she said, coming forward again and offering Raymond her bloodied face. 'Do it,' she insisted to the dismay of Jack, whose hands were over his eyes – he couldn't bear the violence. 'Do it and see how good you feel afterwards,' she sneered. She cast a withering glance at his still-clenched fist. 'Do it! Weak, weak man!' she cried, encouraging the swing of his arm.

Jack seized his father's thick hair, spun him away from her and tripped him face down on the garden, crushing the irises that geysered their scent. I wanted to vomit – but my belly was empty.

Apart from the distant applause of the gathering that had witnessed the unveiling of Sir Winston, everything was spookily quiet again. Ginger, Rachael, Craig and Vanessa were stunned that wiry fifteen-year-old Jack had taken a physical stand against his dad, who was pinned by a knee in the middle of his naked spine. 'If you ever,' said the young 'un, through gritted teeth, as he pulled Raymond's head back by the hair, 'ever hit Mum again, you'll answer to me, Dad. D'you get that?' he added, giving the hair in his fingers an extra hard tug. 'You'll answer to me. You *never*,' he hissed, into Raymond's lughole, 'you *never* hit Mum again.'

Then he stood clear of Raymond, who, lifting himself from the smashed irises, his hairy skin dotted with fragments of yellow, blue and purple petals, asked if Jack was a big man now. The question, with its undertone of violence begetting violence, had his son looking for support from Craig and Rachael, who stared from the upper window as if everything depended on him not caving in to Raymond's cunning – yet oddly loving – empathy.

Ginger let out a moan. Now she needed to save her drunken husband from himself. And, of course, from Jack, whose glare challenged her to defect to the one who had just smashed her nose. 'Oh, for God's sake, Jack,' she said eventually, snorting blood as she brushed past him to join Raymond on her destroyed postage stamp of a garden. 'He's your *father*. You could have hurt him.'

Raymond straightened his back, his wounded tone giving me the jitters when he tried to do right by Jack: 'It's okay, my dear. The boy meant no harm, I'm sure.'

But Jack's brow was as severe as the black stone kerb on which Raymond had nearly damaged himself. 'I meant it, Dad. It's over. The violence. It's over. And you,' he continued, switching his attention to his mum, 'you don't have to go at him when he's drunk. You just don't *have* to,' he ended.

Ginger seemed contrite.

Raymond patted his unclothed hips and breast for a hanky, then selected a light blue iris head with which he clumsily dabbed Ginger's bloodied nostrils. It was a pantomime of apology that drew a smile from his wife, who made a protective fan of her hand where his dangly bit was shrivelled and vulnerable. 'Come on, Ray,' she said, leading him through the Liquorice Allsort, 'we'll clean up.'

26

Rachael caught Jack's attention by loudly clearing her throat and nodding to where the copper – who must have witnessed Raymond getting his comeuppance in the irises – stood at the gate, his hand coming off the walkie-talkie that was clipped to his uniform. Perhaps he was thinking better of contacting the station.

Young Rachael was startled into letting go of the unweighted sash. This time it hit Craig's head. A short but colourful exchange resulted, while the older twins shared a resigned smile that rid the air of some of its tension.

'Everything under control?' asked the copper, who was in his mid-forties and big.

His kindly brown eyes rested on Jack, who retorted, 'Yeah,' and then, remembering his manners, added, 'Thank you very much, Officer.'

'Well,' the copper said, and gave each of the kids a look that was friendly but serious, 'they call me Harris – or Bill, if it suits. Any problems you can't manage, you bring them to me. Deal?' he asked, putting a bit of force into his voice.

'Yes,' agreed Rachael and Craig, quickly. I wondered if they thought any hesitation would mean handcuffs all round.

'Thank you,' smiled Vanessa, clearly relieved that there would be no trouble with the law for Raymond.

'Deal,' agreed Jack, who was giving off so much green that if I'd been a vegetarian my mouth would have watered.

'Everything under control then,' decided Bill, the copper, and gave Jack a respectful nod as he turned to stroll back to where the Salvationists were getting started with 'Onward Christian Soldiers'.

'*Blimey!*' exhaled Jack, staring after him, as the Mayor and his gathering sang of Christians marching to war.

'*Blimey!*' he said to Craig and Rachael, who were side by side at the upper bay, with the broken sash resting across their shoulders.

'*Blimey!*' He shrugged at Vanessa, who carefully lowered her window while giving him a look of pride.

'*Blimey!*' he exclaimed, lifting his big green eyes to the clear blue sky, as if he couldn't believe what he'd just done.

'*Blimey! Blimey! Blimey!*' he cried, as my second sight closed and I woke to find him sitting beside me on the floor, his gaze fixed on his completed Elvis canvas.

'Well, Brucie boy, I just hope Big Eddie likes it,' he said.

Big Eddie who? I wondered, as I marvelled at the strength of character I'd confirmed in Jack.

27

Ginger called through the house, 'I'm back! I've been to the bank! I've shopped! And I've even booked Brucie for the vet for tomorrow! Come on, Artful Bugger, wherever you are!' she added, getting me to make a big bark, which amused Jack. Already into the family way of repeating everything, I did several more as I bounded downstairs to where she was crouched specially for me, just beyond the mahogany newel post. I was unable to report all that I'd discovered of the kids so I made do with slapping my biggest licks on to her joyous face, wishing I could repair where Raymond's fist had bashed her nose out of shape.

'He loves you, Mum,' announced Jack, from the top of the stairs.

'He loves us all,' said Vanessa, poking her head out of the front room (then wasn't the moment to show her mum she was wearing the gold velvet curtain).

'Of course he does,' agreed Rachael, who was all sweaty – she'd probably done another three thousand press-ups. 'And we love him too, thanks, Mum,' she added.

Runaway joy, that prompted Ginger to call me a wonderfully affectionate dog; her green eyes contained depths of gratitude that stirred the love that had come into my heart for her and the kids, a hugeness of feeling that, until then, I hadn't believed possible. It left me doubly determined to understand Craig. Because, of them all, his colour – his *non*-colour – was the dodgy white of a life that might spin in any direction. Why?

Ten minutes later, Ginger was rubbing pink lotion into my sore skin. I would have growled if Picasso the parrot hadn't entranced me by being unashamedly priapic (as if his daydreaming took him beyond his cage on top of Ginger's rusty old fridge).

Anyway, done with my mange, she washed her hands and left me while she put fruit and sugar into a heavy saucepan (I'd soon learn that it was kept for the jam-making she did every summer). She added water and transferred it to the gas ring, then opened the back door on to a long yard packed with metal dustbins planted with ferns made extra green by the sun: a magic forest that almost took my breath away.

'Go on, then,' she urged. 'Keep my boy company.'

I was puzzled because I couldn't see him. Then I looked through the magic forest to where the rear wall of an old building had a partly open wooden door done the same black, grey and pink as the Liquorice Allsort.

'That's it, Brucie,' Ginger encouraged me, getting me started on my first trip to the kid's workshop. 'Make him happy for me. And don't pee on my ferns!' she called

I cocked my leg where a particularly big plant was in a bin with '20 Sea View' painted on its side.

'Oh, you artful bugger!' she cried, as I padded towards the workshop with my hairless tail up like a half-moon, which it had hardly done at all while I was my first human's Runt.

29

The moment I nosed through the partly open door I was struck by how light the workshop was: the flat roof had been replaced with semi-clear plastic sheeting – it was a big window. My next thought was that, in the event of fire, molten bits would do wicked things to Craig's smooth olive skin. If you're thinking I'd looked straight to the bad side, the fact is, the place was *stinking* hot.

Apart from the sun coming through every inch of the roof, the kid – who was wearing the same black T-shirt, blue jeans and scuffed brogues that he'd come to the kennels in – was on his knees, not fixing bicycles, but welding a strip of steel to the side of a big red car. The blue-flamed welding torch and the metal it liquefied gave off an immense heat.

But the second thing that allowed so much light in was that the wide up-and-over door at the front of the building was agape to the rear of the terrace across the lane. It offered an easy escape route if there was a leak in the two skinny rubber tubes that were coloured red for the highly inflammable acetylene, and black for the equally dodgy oxygen. The tubes were taped together and snaked over the floor as one, all the way from the gas cylinders to the aluminium welding torch, which Craig handled with such skill. I kept my presence to myself. Observing him at work was a route to understanding his contrary nature. So advanced with cars. And so lost within himself.

30

B ut I'd only been observing for a minute when a man in the little hotel directly over the lane started singing 'Are You Lonesome Tonight?'. He got louder and nearer until the sneck on his dark green back gate went click and he came into view, ducking so he didn't wreck his quiffed black hair on the stone lintel.

He wasn't just tall: he was a man-mountain, with a small and very round head atop a broad frame that carried a lot of muscle and a generous amount of fat. As he crossed the lane his belly wobbled under his shimmery turquoise shirt; the gold medallion dangling from his short thick neck was as bright as the sun. Or so it seemed. Because if it really had been like that I couldn't have looked at it. He was a sight for my increasingly sore eyes.

Especially when you consider that with his gold-stitched black trousers he wore a shiny black leather belt, with a large rectangular brass E for the buckle. A highly polished adornment that was pulled into his big belly as he bent over Craig's head to see how the welding was going. 'Brilliant!' he boomed. 'A brilliant job by a brilliant laddie!'

Grinning as if he'd won an Olympic medal, Craig finished the last half-inch of the job and closed the valves on the welding torch, which he put aside to cool. 'Thanks, Big Eddie,' he said. He'd confirmed that the man-mountain – who was about forty – was *the* Big Eddie Jack had referred to in connection with his painting of Elvis Presley.

Whipping off his welding goggles and getting up as quick as a arrow from where he'd been kneeling to do his work, he told Big Eddie that once the restoration was complete, he would look amazing in the red car. It was a flash American Ford Mustang, with a front like a grinning shark, although right then it was skew-whiff where the side being welded was lifted on a hydraulic jack with a long T-shaped handle. A careless human could have tripped and bashed his face (that had me worried all over again until I decided the kid was too agile to be tumbling in his own workshop).

By now Big Eddie had copped sight of me, sitting a little way off by the gas cylinders. Craig followed the direction of his friend's quizzical look, his face lighting with joy as he saw that *I* was in his workshop. 'It's the one and only gorgeous Brucie darling!' he declared. Uncertainly he glanced at Big Eddie, who was ogling me as if I was a plucked turkey on the run from Fanny Cradock, almost tapping into my feelings of being useless and ugly: the Runt that should have been drowned.

Except that, with the combined speed of every Ford Mustang ever built, the kid was down low and facing me. His eyes were panda-like – the tight-fitting welding goggles had left dark grooves around the sockets. 'The one and only Brucie darling who's brought his big heart to cheer us all up,' he added, while gently stroking between my eyes, which strayed back to Big Eddie, whose very blue eyes were getting wet at the kid's way of going on with me.

Next thing, Big Eddie came close and tried a version of the name that I already felt had been mine for ever. 'Brucie-Bruce,' he said, and my ears went pathetically flat. It was a response that Ginger would have called artful, but I'd no more control over it than I'd had over my lip-curl at Jack in the kennels.

Still, I must have been a funny sight. Because what did Big Eddie do next but laugh and squeeze the kid's shoulders, remarking that I needed new hair or I'd be jailed for streaking – as Rachael had feared for Raymond after his naked petitioning of the Salvationists.

Suddenly I was savagely depressed – I was easily knocked – as if I didn't simply have soon-to-be-cured mange and conjunctivitis but was without doubt the ugliest and vilest creature on the entire planet. Something so repulsive that Psycho Vet would have done everybody a favour by offing me. I almost clamped my teeth around one of my paws, after all – though I could have got started on my red-raw skin with my ultra-sharp claws. I'd never been walked properly so they hadn't worn down. Each rip of my flesh a punishment for bringing my disgusting self to Ginger and the kids, who needed a dog worthy of them.

Then, looking into my eyes, Craig took my face between his hands, as if he understood the plummeting of my heart. He told me that my sore skin would heal, and my hair would come right, in a flurry of words. Big Eddie clearly regretted what he had said because he scrubbed the kid's head and said I'd be a smashing looker in no time. Then he gave me a more serious appraisal, absently turning his extra wide gold wedding ring on his finger as he declared that mine were eyes you could trust. Like a human's, they were the windows to my soul – a statement that struck me later as canny, coming from a human who had never kept a mutt in his life. 'Yup, Craig lad,' he said, at least three times that I recall, 'eyes you can trust, that dog. Got yourself a pal there already,' he added. I was a good-looking dog for a good-looking laddie, he said.

31

A sharp whine filled me with dread, as if it foretold some terrible thing. You'll have heard about mutts that go mad whenever it's stormy, and one day lightning strikes the house – it's as if they were warning their humans all along. That whine had me cowering behind Craig's compressor for spraying paint. There, I shook as if I was plugged into the mains – I could almost hear Her Hoityness ordering me to get a grip because I was British (that would have been amusing, with her being an Alsatian).

But French, German, British or bite-size Pekinese, getting a grip was highly unlikely: Craig and Big Eddie were as alarmed as I was.

'Blowback!' thundered Big Eddie, as he shifted with surprising speed to wrap his big hands about the top of the red cylinder.

'Shit! Shit! Shit!' yelped the kid, coming to life after a moment of perplexity. It was every gas welder's worst fear: a blowback of flame from the welding torch, up the tube and into the cylinder that – if not blasted into lethal pieces – could launch itself in imitation of the nuclear missile its shape resembled.

'Shit! Shit! Shit!' yelped the kid again, grabbing the

welding torch from where I'd seen him put it aside to cool. A yellow flame now bloomed where the red tube fed the acetylene through the hollow aluminium handle to a copper tip angled for positioning when welding.

'Open the red valve, Craig lad!' ordered Big Eddie, adding, because he didn't dare take his hands off the cylinder to deal with the torch, 'Now, Craig lad!' Despite how quick everything was, my next impression of the kid was so vivid that it's never dimmed: he held the welding torch in his left hand, mesmerized by the flame. Frozen with terror.

'Open the red valve, Craig lad!' roared Big Eddie.

This time Craig held the welding torch at arm's length while looking at his huge friend. His face showed that he knew we'd be offed if the blowback worsened.

'The red valve, Craig,' said Big Eddie, suddenly as cool as a cucumber. 'Open it, please, son. Now.'

The kid nodded and – keeping the torch at a distance – opened the valve: a move that briefly increased the whine to the intensity you might imagine of a real nuclear weapon departing its silo. A truly wicked sound, accompanied by a burst of flame from the copper tip, which meant that the blowback had cleared without a moment to spare.

'Well done!' exclaimed Big Eddie. He glanced over to make sure *I* was okay, then moved fast to take the welding torch from the shaken kid. 'Clever lad,' he added, feeling the torch and the full length of the red tube for fire inside.

My own fear left me when I saw the devastation on poor Craig's face.

32

Big Eddie's shimmery turquoise shirt had gone dark blue under the arms and in the middle of the front and back with sweat that held the reek of fear. He controlled it for the benefit of the kid.

'Dead, dead lucky,' he advised Craig, and showed him where the screw-on connector from the red tube to the torch had been left loose, allowing acetylene to escape, with fire luckily backing only a short way up the tube to the cylinder. It was a simple error that had the kid loathing himself as I much as I had loathed *my*self when I was compared to the streakers on account of my mangy baldness.

'People are right,' he said glumly, as Big Eddie tightened the iffy connection. 'I am *the* retard. The retard who can't do anything,' he added.

He had escaped death by fire but now he was drowning inside. That got me out from behind the compressor. I sat as upright as I could, my bony tail hitting the ground twenty to the dozen, making Big Eddie – who seemed to understand that I *needed* to reassure Craig – relax and smile to himself. 'Don't be sad,' he told the kid.

'Your welding's the best ever. Just remember to tighten

the connections. Otherwise,' he gestured around the workshop, '*poof!*'

Then he showed his faith in Craig by hanging the welding torch on the metal frame that secured the cylinders. All ready for work to start again, once the kid's nerves had settled. 'Go on, Brucie-Bruce,' he boomed, meaning the time was right for me to wiggle the short distance to Craig, who crouched to face me with his furry caterpillars resting heavily over his worried green eyes.

'Bloody hell, Brucie,' he said, suddenly near to tears. 'It's your first day and I nearly blew you up!'

I stood with the flat of my head pushing where his heart was beating in his chest: a simple but strong connection that got his spirits rising as quickly as they'd fallen. It was a way of being that I was all too familiar with.

'You're a darling and I'm glad you're our dog.' He kissed the top of my head, making me feel like a million dollars for the umpteenth time since Ginger and the kids had come to the kennels. 'Hey!' he exclaimed, as I slyly put what strength I could muster into the push against his chest. 'You'll have me shoved over, ya crazy bloody animal!'

Which, because I loved him dearly and wanted to play, was exactly what I did, much to the amusement of Big Eddie, whom I was also beginning to love.

33

When the sneck on the green gate of the hotel clicked again, my inclination to protect the kid had me tensing like a Whippet ready to race.

'Relax, Brucie-Bruce,' chuckled Big Eddie, whose growing friendliness towards me brought a grin to Craig and added to the golden flow I felt inside myself. A wonderful sensation in which love was turning my experience of my own body into something warm rather than wretched, even though I was having waves of dizziness that went from my tummy to my tail and my head, which was as fuggy as the smoke that had come from the incinerator during my stay at the kennels.

A slightly built human with black hair done in a beehive emerged from the hotel and padded across the lane in white rabbit slippers that contrasted with her maroon trouser suit. The thing that really caught my eye, though, because it confirmed who she was, was an extra wide wedding ring identical to Big Eddie's. 'Hello, lovely,' she said, with a smile that, to my delight, put a bit of red around Craig. It was as if her kindness towards him released a disposition for joy, which I knew somebody had undermined as cruelly as my first human in putting his electric cable to my back.

'Hiya, Viv,' he replied, his cheeks pinking. She raised her shoulders in a long shrug of gentle amusement that gave him time to overcome his bashfulness.

I was impressed by her approach so I looked beyond the rabbit slippers, towering hair and thick mascara to her violet eyes, which were as intelligent as they were kind, like those of her Elvis-loving husband. Later I discovered that some humans regarded him as over the top, but he was as sensitive as a sniffer-dog.

He watched Viv take out a packet of king-size cigarettes and light up, using a snazzy gold lighter with a tall flame that could have messed with the lacquer keeping her hair in place. 'So?' she asked Big Eddie meaningfully while keeping an amused eye on the kid (who shrugged as if the husband-and-wife game now beginning was beyond him).

'So?' Big Eddie replied nonchalantly, as she drew on the king-size: if she wanted the banter she'd come outside for, she'd have to get to the point.

'So?' he repeated, with a wink at Craig while she exhaled in her own good time.

'So?' he tried again, making her laugh and flash her gorgeous eyes in a manner that suggested Round One was hers.

'So?' he boomed, as she picked something from her teeth with a long red fingernail that struck me as a miracle of survival: she must have done loads of donkey work in the hotel, which was called the Heartbreak.

'So . . .' she responded at last, giving me a once-over intended to reassure the watchful kid that she was aware of the new dog he must be dying to show her.

'So,' she repeated, her eyes full of humour as she met Big Eddie's questioning gaze, 'what on earth was all the noise? And no lies,' she warned, giving Craig another calming shrug, as if she knew Big Eddie was going to fib merrily every which way he could.

The question that boomed out of her husband – 'What ya on about now, woman?' – held an exaggerated note of offence.

'I mean, *Edwin*,' she retorted, taking yet another draw and exhaling, 'the whine from this workshop that nearly had the hotel windows in. The most *terrible* screaming whine,' she elaborated, as he pulled a face like a confused clown's, then shook his head at Craig and – to my happy amazement – at me.

'No whine that I heard,' he said amiably. 'You must be hearing things, love.'

That was so cheeky that Viv bit her lip to stop herself laughing again, giving me time to note that, although Big Eddie had a small straight nose, his cheeks were rounded by the fat that also gave him a double chin – but he was still a handsome human.

'Ah,' Viv said. She dropped what was left of her king-size and crushed it beneath one of her rabbit slippers – which were probably more of a fire hazard than her lacquered hair. 'Whatever you say, Eddie love,' she agreed, and did her special shrug at her husband. He had the look of one who knows he's never going to win, but enjoys it that way.

34

'And this', she said, a moment later, with a smile for Craig and me, 'must be the lucky dog.'

'Yup,' responded the kid, now squatting beside me as I faced Viv with my blue moons so wide they stung more than ever. It was a response that had Big Eddie resting one hand on his hip and the other on the red Ford Mustang, his tummy wobbling like jelly as he chuckled at what Ginger would have called my artfulness.

'Ber-rucie-Ber-ruce!' he sang, filling the kid with joy that was matched by Viv's laughter: she had clearly grasped that, in loving Craig, Big Eddie – who didn't care for dogs – was also falling for me.

Her succinct verdict that I was 'cute' was disappointing because the least I'd expected was another comment on my coat's potential for a full recovery. In any case, baldy, scabby and itchy as I was, *cute* was not how I felt. But after she'd lit another king-size and scrutinized me for a minute, she made me feel better by remarking that I seemed an *observant* kind of dog.

Where she was concerned, that was sadly true. As sure as I knew the meaning of the liquid rasp at the edge of her words, I saw that her bantering with Big Eddie was a bond of love as strong as that of swans. And, as we all know, swans never take a second mate when the first dies.

Then, as if she felt uneasy under the clarity of my gaze, she looked at Big Eddie and told him kindly but firmly to go inside and clean the cooker. He sighed at the kid and ducked his perfect quiff beneath the lintel of the green gate; the sneck clicked behind him. 'See you later, Craig lad!' he boomed, when he was out of sight. 'See you later, Brucie-Bruce!' he added, with a boyish laugh that had Viv and the kid smiling at each other as they listened for 'Are You Lonesome Tonight?'. Sure as night follows day, Big Eddie was singing it as he returned to his very own Heartbreak Hotel.

35

Viv allowed a few moments to elapse for us to adjust to the silence that followed Big Eddie's singing. Then she asked Craig, 'Are you *sure* everything's okay, lovely?'

'Fine,' he replied, but there was a tremor in his voice, which showed he knew that if the burning acetylene had backed all the way up the red tube the cylinder really might have launched like a nuclear missile, leaving the oxygen to explode into wicked jags of steel that would have offed himself, Big Eddie and me. A worst-case scenario, which was surely why his face went scarlet as he admitted, 'I mean, there was a problem but Big Eddie sorted it, thanks.'

Viv drew on her cigarette, then looked to where he'd welded the side of the red Mustang. She commented that she would probe no more, on condition that he promised always to be safe when he was working. 'So,' she added sternly, as she turned to face him again, 'don't go promising if you're doing anything careless.'

'I *promise*', replied the kid, with wide-eyed conviction that was truly heartrending, 'that I'll always keep everything safe in this workshop. And', he pledged as Viv smiled at his earnestness, 'that from this day, I'll *always* tighten the

connections properly. Always!' he insisted. He was unaware, of course, that *I* was now determined to sniff
the workshop whenever he was there for leaky acetylene,
as Ginger and everybody else who loved Craig would want
me to.

36

Done with the question of the kid's safety, Viv wiped dust from the side window of the Mustang and peered in at the silver vinyl interior. 'You'll have Eddie more flash than ever,' she said, with a smile that was for herself more than for Craig.

'You'll both be flash! You'll see! The flashest couple in the whole wide world!'

His little speech made me so proud of him that I wished I could tell Her Hoityness all about the kids, who – despite their argumentative ways – were full to the brim with the love that had come from Ginger. Except that Her Hoityness was dead, a cold fact that made me all the more appreciative of Viv, as she stroked the kid's cheek and said that if she and Big Eddie *were* to be Mr and Mrs Flash in the fancy red car maybe they ought to be speedy about it. To which Craig calmly agreed, 'Maybe,' and – to my great joy – was surrounded by a rich green: the surest signal so far that his life could come right.

Then she said she needed him always to look out for Big Eddie. He snuffled, nodded and got a hug, like she was his second mum. It moved me so strongly that, if it wasn't for my iron determination to discover exactly what had made him into the so-called retard, I would have been away with the fairies.

37

Viv had padded back to the Heartbreak Hotel, and the kid was lying on the floor in readiness to weld the front valance of Big Eddie's car. I was sitting with one hindquarter resting against his back. Our closeness made him put the welding torch down and roll over to stroke me. But the shiny green blanks that his protective goggles made of his lovely eyes were disturbing, and I was glad when he returned to his work, leaving me to continue my investigation. To my surprise, considering the heat of the day, I felt cold and damp. Except it wasn't *my* cold and damp: it was Craig's. Because I had now *become* him. This must sound odd, and all I can suggest is that you think of it in light of unhappy humans who say they hear voices inside their heads, or who even claim to have different identities from the one that everybody knows is theirs – distress that we dogs *always* feel in our bones.

Not only do we, too, hear the voices; we also sense the 'different' human that has entered the mind of the one we love (my first human's mind was so tangled that towards the end I found it hardest when he was being loving: it was then that I *really* felt his pain). Anyway, the point is that when a mutt's becoming ill with a fever, his second sight can also go haywire, a typical symptom being that, rather than *visiting* the mind of a human, he actually *becomes* that person.

I should have been alarmed because it usually means the illness that's getting under way is so bad that death is on the cards – which, again, is pretty much the same in humans, whose thoughts wander here and there as they sicken and die. Of course, if I *had* been offed that day, I wouldn't be telling this story, but so that you don't become confused, I need to make one more thing absolutely clear.

Once a mutt has survived the experience of 'being' a human, the memories he has of that time are *always* as if he is that human again. So although I – Brucie the mangy mutt – am at the heart of all that's to come, be ready to hear the story in different voices, starting *right now* with the words of the cold wet kid.

38

Cold and wet because where the semi-clear plastic roof would later be, an old wooden covering let the rain into the gloomy workshop, creating mini-streams on the oil-blackened concrete floor where I was on hand to pass tools to my dad, Raymond. He was sitting in the filthy wet, repeatedly whacking a hammer against a bolt for securing a suspension bush that was out of my sight inside the dark wheel arch of a scrappy dark brown Vauxhall Victor.

'Dad,' I wanted to explain, 'that bolt's too fat for the hole. You'll never get it in.' But, with each whack of the hammer scaring me, I didn't *dare* tell him he'd spent twenty minutes attacking the wrong bit of metal – he must have half realized it anyway.

Then, exactly as my recent experience of his worsening temper in the workshop had taught me he would do, he stopped swearing and hammering and became still. Five long seconds passed before he took his head – his hair was roughed up after his exertions – out of the wheel arch, and turned his bullet-hard blue eyes upon me. 'Well, Craig?' he demanded, holding the too-wide bolt up for inspection.

I protested that I'd handed him the correct bolt. When

he'd dropped it, he'd picked up the wrong one from the clutter on the ground around him. My explanation – because of my fear – came with an embarrassing squeak.

He hurled the hammer down so hard that a spark flew where the concrete got chipped. 'Worthless retard!' he roared, his teeth showing through his unruly beard and moustache. If I'd been close enough, he would have bitten into me and torn away flesh. In reality, it was my insides that he was tearing to pieces. 'Useless, useless retard!' he went on.

I shrank into myself and my head was filled with shadowy spaces: a lonely, no-place feeling that came whenever he turned his anger on me.

'Socket wrench,' he demanded, as the correct bolt slipped into the suspension bush so easily that he hardly needed to look at what he was doing. 'Get it right next time,' he added, as he returned his head to the darkness of the wheel arch. I heard the clicking of the wrench as he tightened the bolt.

'Get it right,' he repeated, but softer, as if he knew it was wrong to attack me when I'd always been his special friend in the workshop, where he did cars because his bad nerves meant he couldn't be an art teacher like Mum was.

'Sorry I passed the wrong bolt, Dad,' I said. Most of all I was sorry that I was so worthless.

39

A few minutes later our Jack called me into the house for a talk with him and Vanessa, who'd taken three of Mum's breakfast chairs from the table and placed them in a semi-circle before the kitchen hearth. Where she sat to the left, Jack sat to the right. I was given the middle one, with the welcome heat of the gas fire making steam come from my brogues and denims.

'Look here, Craig,' began Jack, with a glance at Picasso, who was cocking his head our way, 'I heard the old man having a rant at you. A right tongue lashing,' he added, with a meaningful look at our sister.

A week ago she had told me to stop acting as if the bullying in the workshop didn't matter. Her rebuke had embarrassed me so much that now I lied through my teeth. 'It wasn't a tongue lashing. Me and Dad were joking like always. And if youse must know . . . if he does rant, it doesn't matter one bit.'

Instead of actually looking at *me*, Vanessa sought my eyes in an oval mirror on the chimney breast and said that, however much I denied it, they *knew* that whatever was happening between me and Dad mattered. Jack was also being tricksy with the mirror and he supported what she had said with one of his looks: his head came forward, making his already powerful gaze extra commanding. 'Agreed, our Vanessa,' he said.

'In fact, it matters a lot.'

'Well, not to me!' I snapped, with the anger that came from an ingrained fear that any probing would expose me as a weakling who was scared of shadowy places that didn't exist. Except within his own cracked head. 'So get lost and mind your own business,' I told them. I returned my chair to the table and headed for the back door. It had glass upper and lower panes with condensation inside, and rain out.

'That's right, Craig,' called Jack, who further annoyed me by sounding really adult. 'Crawl back to the workshop and let Daddio walk all over you.'

'Go to Hell!' I retorted.

'Exactly what you should tell *him* to do!' he fired back, via the mirror.

'Ah, but he daren't,' interjected Vanessa, who calmly got up and touched her twin on the shoulder, indicating that he, too, should stand. 'He's terrorized,' she explained, returning their chairs to the table and looking at me with eyes that were kind but just as challenging as my brother's.

'Look! You two reckon you understand *everything* because Jack sorted Dad when he was bollock-naked and punched Mum's nose! Well,' I continued, as they rolled their eyes and Picasso hopped about because things were getting exciting, 'remember that youse are only just sixteen. Not the oh-so-grown-up king and queen of the house!' I spluttered. They smiled between themselves with such fondness that I stamped my foot. 'You see?' I cried, mostly furious with myself because I was unable to prevent a smile of my own. 'Ya mock every bloody thing!'

'Well,' said Vanessa, after a moment of quiet, 'these days, Craig may have a face like he's tripped on a kerb, but at least he's still game for a battle.'

'Oh, he's that all right,' replied Jack, whose gaze slid teasingly to the kitchen mop in its galvanized bucket beside the back door.

I twitched as I calculated that I could probably get to it before him. I was forestalled by Vanessa crying, 'Oh, no, you don't! We're having a serious talk about Dad. Aren't we?' she demanded, looking daggers at Jack, who guiltily bit his lower lip (as he always did, when he was torn between behaving like an adult and having fun with me).

'Okay.' He gave me a look that held the promise of a mop fight to come. 'We'll be serious for now.'

'You'd better,' she cautioned, parking herself in front of the mop in case one of us lunged for it. 'Clowns.'

Jack gave me a wry smile that churned me up inside. Instead of having to be serious, I simply wanted them and me and Rachael, who was in her room doing her training, to be happy. 'The pair of you worry too much!' I declared. I was sort of enjoying myself as I added, 'You'll get ulcers like dustbin lids!'

'Well, maybe we do, and maybe we will,' conceded Jack, with a glance at Vanessa, who shrugged and smiled as he continued, 'But tell us what's really going on with Dad. Please, Craigie.' His now rather sad green eyes found mine again in the mirror, where – because we were standing apart – I was surprised to see the three of us still reflected.

'And *try* not to get annoyed,' advised my sister, who softened my resistance a bit more by remarking that otherwise we might cause Picasso to die of overexcitement.

'Ha!' Jack quipped, as he followed her eyes to where our beady-eyed parrot – who'd been in Mum's family for *fifty years* – was waiting for things to get going again. 'That's a good point, Vee!'

'If we kill *him* off, Mum'll bloody slaughter us!'

Just as quickly Jack became serious again, giving me a marble look that meant the sooner I spilt the beans, the sooner the big-brother/big-sister/little-brother talk would be over – leaving him and me to dive for the stinky mop. It was used for all things disgusting, like when our pee missed the toilet. Which drove our Rachael nuts.

40

Every Thursday evening Dad took me to the car auctions where, because he always swigged from a half-bottle of Bell's, he was known as Mr Bells, and where, on account of my own excitement at finding Cataloy filler on tarted-up cars, I was his deputy, the Cataloy Kid. It was the kind of moniker that makes you feel brilliant when tough blokes in the motor trade say it and you're only ten – though, actually, it started when I was eight and the auctioneer, who fancied himself as a showman, closed the bidding on a dark blue Rover V8; it was identical to Harold Wilson's car, which I'd seen on the news, outside 10 Downing Street.

'Lot number one two two, a performance motor-car with leather and wood, condition, it's true, all very good. Sold to Mr Bells and the one and only Cataloy Kid!'

The fall of the hammer was accompanied by a round of laughter that made me truly proud to be Dad's deputy, especially when he ruffled my hair and saluted to the auctioneer, who was so fast and clear with his phrasing that he'd long since earned a moniker of his own: Dr Mouth.

'Thank you, kind sir,' called Dad, across the bay that the cars were driven onto for the minute or two of their sale. 'A winning performance as usual from Mouth.' He bowed his head this way and that at the surrounding bidders, who now roared with a different laughter – it bordered on revenge against the auctioneer, whom Dad had jovially undermined by removing the 'Dr' from his nickname.

The auctioneer – who wore a black suit and had silver-framed glasses and bony features – was the high priest of the sale: a spruce, arrogant man who sat above the bidders at a red Formica rostrum that shone beneath strip lights positioned to make even the roughest car look better than it was. An elevated post, whence he held sway over the proceedings and, of course, over the bidders, most of whom were overawed by him.

Unlike Dad: he stood straight and steady as he stared across the roof of the blue Rover V8 and up to the rostrum; his big grey beard made him look how I sometimes imagined God to be, because that was how greatly I'd always loved him. My car-fixing superhero of a dad: he made me feel so valued and warm that, no matter how far I strayed from his side, it was as if an invisible artery fed his love to me. But I was a bit embarrassed that some of the other bidders at the Rover V8 sale were seeing a half-cut geezer whose fingers and whiskery lips were stained dark brown by cigarettes – a near-tramp who, despite having seven hundred quid in cash to pay for the Rover, was wearing an overcoat with all the buttons missing so it hung over his belly like half-drawn curtains.

Dr Mouth didn't miss that – and from then on, he was always Dr Death to me. He could have let Dad have his moment of triumph, but he had to try to destroy his dignity.

'Take it away,' he instructed the man who'd driven the Rover into the selling bay. 'Sold to Mr Bells,' he said again, and added, 'Let us pray that he finds some coat buttons in the glove box!'

After that, I was consumed by dread that all the blokes – who were themselves in donkey jackets – were actually jeering at my dad, like he was the joke. Except that back then he was still sharp enough to wangle his way out of most situations. 'Well, *Dr* Mouth,' he called, 'should I do so, *sir*, I'll take them to the button auction and make extra money.' Not a great joke in itself but delivered with swiftness that turned the laughter back against the auction-eer.

He didn't look at Dad as he said, 'Whatever you say, Bells,' and signalled for the next car from the waiting line. He'd let Dad have victory – but I knew he'd only just got away with it, the first time ever that I'd been worried for him at the auctions, where he was known to be magic with cars. If he hadn't drunk too much Bell's whisky.

41

Before I knew it, I'd waxed lyrical and Jack was riveted by my description of the car auction. 'All this time and I knew *nothing* about Mr Bells and the Cataloy Kid!' he exclaimed, looking from me to Vanessa, who was smiling – she knew I was proud at impressing my big brother with talk of an auctioneering high priest and a Rover V8 that was identical to the Prime Minister's car.

'Oh, but *I* knew,' she said – we occasionally had private chats about happier times with Dad. 'Our Craigie's told me loads,' she added.

It was then that Jack announced he was coming to the next car auction. The idea gave me the horrors – it would have been like me going to the City Art Gallery with him and Mum. Each of us kids had a number-one passion that the others didn't get in the way of: cars for me, art for him, clothes for Vanessa and sports for Rachael.

'But come on,' he persisted, as he retrieved the breakfast chairs and got the three of us seated again, 'you can tell me some more, Craigie. Can't he?' he asked Vanessa.

'Don't ask me, ask him,' she teased.

She knew I was even prouder that Jack – who was always up for a fun-fight but usually dismissive of what I had to *say* – was eager to hear more. I told him to give me a moment to think – really, I just wanted to make him wait for once, which had Vanessa remarking, 'I don't know. You two. Priceless as *yin* and *yang*.'

But my mind and tongue were spoiling to get going again – like, now they'd got me started, I *really* needed to talk. I resisted the urge with a scan of the kitchen and felt glad we were sitting away from the mirror, and more than a bit self-conscious at the fun Picasso was having with himself.

'Never mind horny bloody Picasso,' ordered Jack, making my eyes return to him. 'Tell me more about the car auctions. And', he added, reaching over to nip my ear – the sort of tweak we gave each other when we weren't up for a proper fun-fight – 'don't forget we want to know what's gone wrong with you and Dad in the workshop.'

42

I stroked my ear – the nip had hurt – but really I was sneaking a look at Picasso, who had speeded up. The distraction wasn't lost on Jack, who faced me with a funny smile, like he was entertained but wished the flaming parrot would stop rubbing himself against the plastic water-butt clipped to his cage.

'Oh, stop spying on him, you two!' ordered Vanessa, looking at Picasso, who'd suddenly become tranquil. His eye remained on her while she slyly added that his way of going on with himself was harmless enough.

That got Jack – who'd gone as crimson in the face as I suddenly felt hot under the collar – shoving a hand through his wild black hair: a sure sign of annoyance. 'Yes, harmless enough!' he fumed. 'Except that more than once a week causes hairy palms and madness! Very, very Victorian!' he concluded, eyeing me with triumph but blind to my sudden worry at his reference to madness.

'Well,' responded Vanessa, as she ran her eyes from me to him, 'people say these things, don't they? But as for our Picasso – I don't see hairy *claws* or madness. Do you?' she enquired of my brother, who half sighed and half laughed in acknowledgement that, although she was like a nail on a blackboard, our sister was at least witty.

'Very droll,' he said. 'Ha-ha, Vanessa. You see? I'm laughing my titties off! In fact,' he concluded, with a glance that wondered why I wasn't amused by his sarcasm, 'any minute now they're going to drop to the floor, leaving me titless.'

'You mean witless,' came the reply, as she switched her gaze back to me. 'Well, our Craig, what's going on in that funny old head of yours? Something's up,' she insisted, as Jack finally saw that their banter had distressed me.

'What is it?' he asked, as they craned closer, their fat black eyebrows arching high above eyes so full of curiosity that the green had turned the colour of spinach, a funny times-four effect that had me looking at the floor in case I laughed when they were trying to be kind.

'Come on,' they urged, even keener now to know what I was thinking.

'Well . . .' I stalled because I knew I was about to make myself look ridiculous, but I needed to get rid of the worry that was making my belly fizz like it did when Dad shouted horrible things into my face. 'Well, the thing is . . . our Picasso doesn't have hairy claws – but he does pull his feathers out! I mean, just look at him!' He'd long since plucked bare his chest, under his wings and parts of his back. 'Look! Look! Look at him!' I cried, indignant that Jack and Vanessa were now bent double with laughter that forced me to raise my voice. 'He's like a plucked chicken! And only a *mad* parrot', I stressed as hard as I could, 'would pluck himself!'

Jack said something funny about the word 'pluck', and I became so frustrated by their laughter that I jumped up and down on the spot. 'Well, if it's so funny, Mr and Mrs Clever Bloody Clogs, why does he do it?' I demanded, genuinely wanting to know. '*Why?*' I heard myself bellow. It was as if I was two people, one listening as the other became hysterical enough to jolt my sister and brother out of their high spirits. Silence entered the room as quickly as a dropped brick.

'Steady on, little bro,' advised Jack, whose eyes now held the reassuring expression that came when he knew I was out of my depth.

'There's no need to get *so* upset,' added Vanessa.

I splurged out that all I'd been trying to say was, our Picasso was as baldy as Kojak off the telly because he suffered from madness that made him pluck his feathers. And that he was mad in the first place because – well, they knew what he was always doing with his plastic water-butt! That had Jack half sighing and half laughing again. He asked Vanessa to put my mind at rest before I *was* taken away by men in white coats.

'Sweet daft little brother,' she said, 'the simple reason that Picasso plucks his feathers is because he's stuck in a flipping cage.'

'And not', concluded Jack, 'because he's gone crackers through *incessant* plonker pulling! Now,' he added, eyeballing me, 'the workshop and Dad.'

None of us kids ever gave in to the others too easily. For the sake of my standing within the family, I acted like I was still annoyed at being pressured to tell them about the workshop situation.

'All right, bloody tyrants,' I eventually grumbled. 'Give me a mo to gather my thoughts and I'll tell youse everything.'

'Why not just hurry up before Dad calls you back outside?' Vanessa suggested.

'Yeah, come on, man, Craigie,' urged Jack. 'By the time you get started our Picasso will have regrown his feathers.'

'Okay,' I agreed, unable to disguise my happiness that they really *did* want to hear my tale. It came with a speed that surprised me . . .

43

The last time it was great was when Dad stole a 1970 Mk II Cortina 1600E from Dr Death for a hundred and fifty quid. We knew the car already, and I can even remember when it was brand new to a man who owned one of the small hotels at the far end of the seafront. God, it was so beautiful. They were like the poor man's Rolls-Royce. Comfy seats. Wooden dashboard and door cappings – really highly polished, with a gorgeous grain to the timber. Plus dead stylish sports wheels, called Ro-styles, and a leather-rimmed steering-wheel: fantastic cars that sent the blood whacking through your veins. Or, leastways, they do through mine. And the thing is, this one was a rare pale metallic pink called Light Orchid. A colour that suits the neat lines of the Mk II like it's almost invisible: not fancy, just exquisite. Totally beautiful.

The first day I saw it, it was outside the hotel, gleaming in the sun with the silver blue sea behind. One of the best things I'd ever seen. A vision. A sculpture. A work of art. In fact, I even took Dad along; we went in a dark blue '63 Morris Oxford that'd got rotten sills and the back exhaust missing. Great fun. Sounded like the Russians had arrived. Then Dad said the car I'd taken him to see showed that, even though I was only nine, I had 'discernment' – afterwards I looked that word up in the dictionary and felt really special.

The hotel man didn't value what he'd got and it was always mucky inside and out, especially in winter with the salt, which was making the back wheel arches and front wings go rusty. It's amazing how quickly that happens. Makes you want to cry. Sometimes I used to write messages in the dirt on its bonnet when I was doing my paper round – 'Save me! You're letting me rust to death!' that sort of thing. Mad, really, I suppose.

Then it turned up at the auction, which didn't surprise me because I'd already told Dad that the hotel man had got a horrible new Daytona Yellow Mk III Cortina, which showed how much 'discernment' he had. Dad laughed, but told me not to get above myself.

Obviously it had come via the trade, which was how it worked. The posh dealers did the new stuff, sent the trade-ins to the auctions, and the next lot of dealers tidied them up and sold them on, most from forecourts but some from back lanes, like Dad.

The likes of me and Dad bought the trade-ins at the forecourts as well; Dad said that was a case of little fish eating off the backs of whales. Anyway, I was thrilled because my one and only chance to save the car from rusting away had come on a plate – though when you looked dead close, the arches and wings weren't that rotten, and the special badges and trim bits were all there. And it only had thirty-nine thousand miles on the clock. Hardly run in. But terrible to look at: the paint had turned a dull salmon colour that was rough to touch where the aluminium flecks that created the metallic effect were corroded.

Bid for it, I told Dad. It's a heap, he said. And the embarrassing thing was, I actually got tears in my eyes, which some of the trade blokes saw. Bid for it, I kept saying. And even though I'd always loved the car, and once said a prayer to God for it to be rescued from the hotel man, afterwards I was puzzled by how much it meant to me. If we hadn't got it, it would have been like somebody had died or something. I can't describe it without sounding crazy. I just burned to polish it back to the fabulous colour it'd once been, which Dad said was impossible without giving it a respray.

But the more he said it, the more determined I was. *He* might not have been able to save the paintwork, but *I* could. In the end he said that if we bought it and lost money I had to give him my paper-round cash until it was made up again. Didn't bother me. I knew I could make that car beautiful. And even Dad was surprised when Dr Death knocked it down at one fifty. It put him in such a good mood that he announced it was *my* project to make it gleam again. And if you'd asked me then, I would have said that the sun was going to shine out of Dad's bum for ever.

44

Vanessa smiled at Jack, who was watching me with interest. My words had left me breathless. 'My God, Jack,' she said, with a lovely laugh. 'Our little brother's first love was a pink car! No wonder he worries about madness!' she concluded.

I arched my eyebrows, like they were always doing with theirs. 'What's so wrong about that?' I demanded. 'At least it wasn't a crappy Mk III Cortina. Or a plastic water-butt,' I added.

Picasso was watching us like he understood everything we were saying.

'Never mind first love and all that,' Jack said. 'What happened next, Craig?'

'Vim and Brasso,' I answered proudly.

Their eyebrows went up again.

45

'First off, I got Mum's Vim from the bog and mixed it with a splash of water. Just enough to make an abrasive paste for taking the corrosion off the aluminium in the metallic paint. Stage two was to do every bit of the car again, but with shampoo in the paste, making it creamier, softer. That put the shine back on the bits of aluminium where I'd polished away the corrosion. Then I did a panel at a time with Brasso, which removed the scratches the Vim had put into all the pinkness. By now the surface was becoming smooth and shiny, with the proper colour returning. I got excited: I was rescuing something beautiful.

'After that, I washed the car with scalding hot water and loads of Mum's Fairy Liquid. Big white bubbles on the gleaming Light Orchid that I'd brought back to life, with the rust on the arches and wings hardly showing when the brown staining was polished away. Just to protect the mirror surface I'd brought back, I waxed the whole thing three times.

'Next, I did the Ro-style wheels with aluminium paint and cleaned the tyre walls with brake fluid. I made the glass and chrome sparkle, and buffed the interior, which came up perfectly – the poor man's Rolls-Royce reborn! Luckily enough, it even *smelt* clean because the hotel man hadn't been a smoker, which really knackers a car inside.

'So there you go. I'd saved the 1600E that I'd worried about for years. My best, *best* car moment ever. A brilliant feeling. Poor old Dad stood back, looked at the car gleaming in the sun, and couldn't believe his eyes. And with Dr Death's auction commission and all the cleaning stuff counted – most of which we'd nicked from Mum – it was still under two hundred quid! Magic, magic, magic!'

46

Even though it was months since I'd made the car shine again, all the excitement had returned as I'd told the tale to my brother and sister, taking me to where I could almost feel the slippery surface of the silvery-pink bodywork beneath my fingers. A rich and happy sensation that Jack shattered by asking, 'And what exactly did *Daddio* say? . . . C'mon, Craig,' he insisted.

I avoided his eyes. His question was making me relive the onset of the rages that had branded me as the one and only retard I knew of. It was a horrible fact of life that I'd prayed to God to let no one but Dad see the ugly truth about me. Because only He could have forgiven me for whatever I'd done to become so despicable, so loathsome, a repugnant creature who had driven his own father – he'd never before been angry with us kids – to turn on him. It was a wicked distortion of our dad that I knew *I* was the cause of. It was all the more terrifying when he shouted, 'Worthless little retard! Worthless little retard! Worthless little retard!' Horrible, horrible words that *I* had driven him to. Because I was wicked. And dirty. Like he sometimes said. A worthless, dirty little *thing* who couldn't even speak up when he knew his tired old dad was trying to hammer the wrong bolt into the suspension of a scrappy brown Vauxhall Victor.

That was me. A worthless, dirty runt – and only Dad knew the truth because he was the person I spent the most time with. Maybe it was because of me that he had been drinking more in recent months.

Help me to be good, God, I'd prayed. And, please, please, don't let my family see what a vile and despicable creature I really am. Keep that away from our Vanessa, Jack and Rachael. Keep that away from Mum. Keep that between me and Dad and I'll do everything I can to get clean again. Please, please, God. I swear on my life that I didn't mean to cause the trouble that's come.

Such were the things that whirled within me, as if, all of a sudden, I was going to be sucked under by the thoughts and feelings that had started when I'd first made Dad angry, thoughts and feelings that'd robbed me of my joy and brought sadness that became stronger and stronger and stronger. Punishment because I was a disgusting thing, even if I didn't know how or why I'd become so. A boy who had made his superhero dad – who was magic with the cars they both loved – hate him.

Vanessa threw me a lifeline. She must have seen I was drowning in feelings I couldn't control. 'Please, Craig,' she said, 'Jack only wants to know what Dad said when he saw the car polished up. Don't you, our Jay?'

My brother relaxed his eyes, which had been really wide and intimidatingly spinach-coloured. He even managed a smile – which he rarely did when in one of his really serious moods.

'Ah!' I exclaimed, seeing a way to avoid saying just how mightily disgusted Dad had become with me. 'He was dead chuffed! Gave me a fiver and said I was a clever lad! First time he'd ever paid me for helping him!'

'You mean,' retorted Jack, '*the one and only time*. Five miserable bloody quid,' he added, with a glance at Vanessa.

She hadn't been fooled either by my lively manner. 'C'mon, Craigie.'

'I'm not mucking around!'

'How *did* things pan out?' Jack asked, again sounding so adult that I felt my pride in what I'd achieved with the car was under attack. It was the same as me praising one of his paintings, then turning it upside-down and saying it looked better that way.

'It was his best deal ever!' I protested, hating the tears that were in my eyes for making me look weak. 'His *very best* deal!' I shouted, determined they should acknowledge that I hadn't only saved the Light Orchid Cortina but that Dad had pulled off a good bit of business. 'Six hundred and eighty-five quid he got! Can you believe it?' I was relieved and cheered that they were grinning between themselves. 'A mark-up of four hundred and eighty-five!' I added. I was genuinely thrilled all over again. Perhaps I – *the retard* – was worth something after all. '*Four hundred and eighty five quid!*' I sang, in the funny voice that Dad used when he was being playful with Vanessa (who always brought out the best in him). '*Four hundred and eighty-five quid, Mr Pablo Picasso!*' I trilled a finger across the rusty bars of the cage, awakening our baldy old pet from the snooze that'd followed his activity with the water-butt. *'Four hundred and eighty-five quid! And all down to me!'* I crooned, shooting a look at the mop. I decided against attacking my brother with it just yet.

'Four hundred and eighty-five quid profit!' I sang on, taking my voice higher and giving Jack's ear a nip, which brought a satisfying yelp. Vanessa's laugh inspired me to climb on to Mum's breakfast table and gesture like an opera singer. *'Four hundred and eighty-five quid profit!'* I yodelled, aware that while Jack and Vanessa were throwing their arms up in happy protest at the racket I was making, Picasso was again becoming lively with himself.

'Four hundred and eighty-five quid profit!' I repeated yet again, only this time easing back on my voice as I stepped off the table via a breakfast chair that creaked: a warning of damage to its frame that had me quickly shifting my weight.

'Four hundred and eighty-five quid,' I said calmly, as I met their amused eyes while folding my arms and wiggling my bum to test the chair, which didn't seem to be weakened, after all.

'Four hundred and eighty-five quid!' mimicked Picasso, astonishing us all.

47

But they knew I'd evaded the question of what had changed between me and Dad. So when we'd stopped laughing at Picasso, they demanded answers.

'Do youse never give up?' I asked.

'I don't know,' replied Jack. 'Do we ever give up?' he enquired of Vanessa, whose smiling advice was that I should consider them as determined as a Rottweiler with a bone.

'Ha!' I cried, pointing at my brother's great clump of black hair. 'Ha!' I repeated, aiming the same finger at where Vanessa's equally dark hair was done in rough spikes (she got rid of them when punk rock came because we *never* followed trends). 'Ha!' I cried yet again, narrowing an eye like Detective Columbo. 'A Rottweiler has beautiful hair whereas youse have straw. Except', I added, my idiot tongue running away with me because I knew they were going to make me talk, 'it's the wrong colour!'

'Well,' responded Jack, drily, 'you can always dye it yellow when we're asleep.'

'And then', suggested Vanessa, even more drily, 'we'll be the Wurzel Gummidge twins.'

'But meanwhile', persisted Jack, 'you can tell us what the hell's been going on.'

My sister agreed.

I retorted that, whatever they *thought* I was going to do, they couldn't have been the Wurzel Gummidge twins because they were too ugly. They laughed with a fondness that had me suddenly *wanting* to tell them everything. Especially how dirty I was. An inclination I overpowered. Who would want to face filth like mine?

Vanessa slumped her shoulders and her eyes went doe-like. 'Listen, our Craig, we don't want to bully you. In fact, we remember the day you finished the pink car.'

'Light Orchid.' I flicked a glance at Jack that was meant to disguise the fact that her reference to my special car had got me hooked, though it was my brother who recalled that even Mum and Rachael had come out to see the shine I'd put back on the paintwork.

'Hey!' he exclaimed, as if he was only just remembering. 'Big Eddie loved it so much his mate bought it!'

'Correct!' I confirmed. I was so chuffed at the inclusion of Big Eddie that I didn't see Jack's cunning when he asked if I remembered who had ticked us off for laughing at the Elvis thing when Big Eddie and Viv had opened the Heartbreak Hotel a year before.

'Dad!' broke in Vanessa, while I was lost in guilt that I'd once laughed at my kind friends from across the lane. '*Dad!*' she emphasized, her posture back to normal. Her eyes flashed as she protested, 'And, for God's sake, no more evasions, Craig! You're not the only one in this family – he's

122

our father too! We want to know about him for us as well as for you! Tell him that's right,' she ordered Jack.

Before he could say anything, I was spilling beans so fast it's a wonder I didn't slip on them.

48

'What happened was, Dad started drinking more than usual and at the same time kept looking at me as if there was something angry he couldn't say. Like a rumbly volcano, without the big blow-up actually happening.

'Then at the car auctions – where the blokes had already been laughing about how drunk he was – a Corsair 2000E came through. Like a bigger version of the Cortina 1600E but not as good, especially when they've got more rot than the *Titanic*. Which was exactly what any boozed-up maniac on a galloping horse could see was the problem with this piece of junk. Plus it'd had a colour change from light metallic blue to glossy black, with its original vinyl roof covered in over-spray.

'But Dad – drunk for days – bloody Dad wanted to make a bloody point. If I could do the 1600E, he could do the 2000E: "Another four hundred and eighty-five quid mark-up!" he reckoned, but really savage. Like he *hated* me for what I'd done. The first time *ever* that he'd turned on me like that.

'Then he was bidding as if his flipping life depended on it, with Dr Death, in his perfect dark suit and silver glasses, going like the clappers, and some of the blokes tossing bids in just to see how far Dad would go. It was mad! Because soon he was up to five hundred! Five hundred quid for a car worth a hundred, absolute tops!

'And then some of the blokes were jeering and laughing at *our* dad, who was trying to do the happy clowning he does with Vanessa, except that looking at him, he was exactly that: a big, scruffy, smelly clown. Laughed at. Mocked. And with all the 1600E money we'd made getting wasted on the effing 2000E that was so knackered it wasn't even firing on four cylinders.

'I *hated* that car. Hated it on sight. Hated Dr Death for driving Dad on. Hated the blokes for kicking him when he was down and – *almost* – hated Dad for being so crazy when we had the cash to buy good cars and do good things. Because that's how it starts. A few good deals that lead to more deals, lucky breaks and savvy all mixed up. Dad had no savvy left. He was mad. And getting really, really angry when he was realizing that they were laughing *at* him, not *with* him.

'"Five hundred and eighty!" bid one of the blokes, just to make him go further. '"Seven hundred!" bid Dad, quick as lightning.

'To be fair, some of the blokes turned their backs, but most were enjoying it. Same as watching a dog-fight where one is going to die, blood all over, adding to the excitement for those who have placed bets. Horrible. Horrible. Horrible. So horrible that, for a while, I couldn't look at the red-coloured rostrum because, with all the bright lights, it was like Dad's blood was being let. And he was dying. That very night. That was true in a way. Because afterwards he was never Mr Bells again. He was Old Boozy, the biggest laughing stock on two pissed legs.

'And as for Dr Death, he kept his stupid little silver hammer poised and looked from Dad to the other bidder, the one who'd gone five eighty and made Dad do seven. "Any further bids on seven?" he asked, in his wicked, clear voice. "Any further bids on seven?" he said again, playing it like an ordinary sale when really he was teasing everybody, with Dad in the middle, a crazed old dog who wouldn't give up, even though he was bitten and bleeding all over.

'"Any further bids on seven?" repeated Dr Death, still looking at the other bidder, who was too savvy to up the stakes in case Dad came to his senses and made *him* into the mug who'd bought a massively overpriced car.

'Then Dr Death was doing his selling once, selling twice thing and Dad went and upped his own bid to eight hundred. At first I thought he'd gone really crackers, but then saw what he was about: eye to eye with Dr Death across the roof of the car, he'd got some kind of savvy back, bidding, "Eight ten . . . Eight twenty . . . Eight thirty . . . Eight forty . . ." thereby getting most of the blokes to turn against Dr Death, who for once was flustered.

'The high priest of the sale was suddenly right down low. Where, if ya ask me, he deserved to be. Like a worm. But worms do good, and he was cruel and flinty and, because of what he did to Dad, worse than something you wipe off your shoe. But then – and this is the bit I hate most – Dr Death wasn't the only one who'd lost his way.

'Where Dad had had the upper hand and was carrying on with his "Nine ten . . . Nine twenty . . . Nine thirty . . ." and basically slaughtering Dr Death, I wanted the ground to open up and swallow me. Except that the opposite happened and I blew up like a volcano, shouting that Dad didn't mean it and he was sorry for all the trouble he'd caused. Words that just spewed out because I was scared that Dad *had* gone totally crackers, even if he was getting back at Dr Death, who seized my apology with one word – accepted – and brought his little hammer down with a whack that meant the shitty hundred-quid car was ours for nearly a grand!

'The whole place – beyond the sale area and into the big looming show halls – was ice-quiet again, with all eyes on me where I'd humiliated Dad by apologizing for him when I was only the Cataloy Kid, and he'd been doing car auctions since before I was born. But the eyes I was terrified of were his. Dad's. Cold, hard eyes that hated. Really, really *hated.* With the extra scary thing being that there was no way I could snaffle back what I'd gone and said.

'"1970 Corsair 2000E. Sold for nine hundred and sixty pounds," announced Dr Death, rubbing salt into Dad's wounds, my wounds, and any other wounds anywhere in the hall. "Take it away," he said. All the time Dad was looking down on me like I was something that needed to be wiped off *his* shoe. Then he said *exactly* what was on his mind. The stuff he'd felt ever since I'd done so well with the Cortina that had made us four hundred and eighty-five quid profit.'

49

Rain was still hitting the glass of the back door, but a break in the sky cast a silvery light that the mirror on the chimney piece reflected into the bit of kitchen behind Jack and Vanessa. They faced me with a glumness that made me wish I hadn't got so carried away about the disastrous night at the car auctions.

'Poor Dad,' sighed my sister, breaking the hush as she looked down at the lino, which had tiny yellow seahorses on a blue background.

'Never mind *him*,' said Jack, his face like a robot's: he was determined not to be swayed by pity for Dad. 'What did he actually *say* to you, our Craig?' he asked.

My neck went hot and my belly was fizzy again. My runaway tongue had led me dangerously close to revealing the truth of my own filthy nature: a revelation that would have been sure to wipe out all the love my brother and Vanessa had for me. The same as had happened with Dad: now he only sent disgust down the invisible artery that had once brought love to wherever I was.

'C'mon, our Craig,' Jack demanded, his voice rising, as I became hotter, fizzier and more bothered. 'C'mon! C'mon!' he barked.

Vanessa lifted her eyes from the seahorses and arched an eyebrow at him.

'We've come this far, our Vee! We're not stopping now! What did Dad actually *say*?'

'I don't know,' I lied, hoping to make him back off by sounding upset, yet surprised by the girly pitch of my voice – the effect of terror.

'Then try and remember,' he urged.

He didn't know that behind the gaze with which I met his I saw Dad's hate-filled eyes. Eyes that had been boring into me ever since the night when all the blokes from the trade, plus Dr Death and his assistants, and even the ladies who sold tea near the red rostrum, had heard what he'd said: his voice neither loud nor quiet, just steady, clear, and without any of the slurring that was usually there when he was drunk.

Words that had been thought about and shaped in his mind, and that came with all the purpose of a man digging a grave, as if after the humiliation I'd brought him, he was justified in burying me. Not that I could blame him, with what I knew about myself.

'You little shit,' he began, making me feel exactly that, although I was still scrabbling to believe that he didn't mean what he was saying to *me*, the one and only Cataloy Kid, who'd always been his special friend.

'But, Dad—'

In the same hard voice he overrode me, making my eyes burn with tears as he said the words that cut into my soul. Words of a type that I'd long feared with every bit of my being.

At school they had names for lads like me. Marcus Wright from my class had gone stiff in the showers after PE and got bullied so badly that he took his mum's sleeping pills. Because I was scared of getting found out, I'd joined those who'd spat upon him and had even slapped bubble gum into his hair.

Later, when he'd been moved to a different school – but was still called Mandy by everybody – and I'd tried to apologize, he'd said he knew all about me, that my turn would come and not to expect him to be around to help because I was scum for what I'd done. And now Dad was spelling it out as well: the truth, with dozens of pairs of ears listening.

'You *worthless* little shit. Do you think I don't *know* what you are? Limp-wristed little *queer*.' He captured everything that dogged my dreams in a single word that froze my blood.

'Cataloy, go home,' advised one of the blokes, as Dad lurched off through the silent crowd to pay for the overpriced car that festered beneath its glossy paint.

50

'I know what he said!' exclaimed Vanessa, rescuing me from my memories of the car auction, yet filling me with dread that, like Dad, she'd realized I was a queer. 'He said in front of all those people at the auction that you were the retard, didn't he?' She was nodding during the moments it took me to grasp that another lifeline had been thrown my way.

'Of course!' cried Jack, who – always quick to understand his twin's motives – tweaked my nose.

I gave an exaggerated 'Ouch' that got them laughing so hard I wondered later if they were relieved that I hadn't told them the truth, whatever it was.

'That's it, the birth of the retard!' I agreed, amazed that I was benefiting from the coded phrase Dad used for my queer vileness. 'And I'll tell youse what,' I continued, on a roll now, 'he's been saying it ever since that night! *Retard!*' I parodied, with vehemence that made me feel hollow. I knew I deserved punishment for being queer, but Dad had wounded me more than I'd admitted to myself.

'Retard,' I concluded, evading the troubled eyes of Jack and Vanessa by looking at our sleepy Picasso, who was perched on one leg.

'Well,' began Jack, as if he was Sherlock Holmes, 'one thing's clear. The workshop *protégé* – that's you, our Craigie – had surpassed the workshop *mentor* even before the auction brouhaha. Agreed?' he asked Vanessa, who said it was obvious that when I'd done so well on the Cortina 1600E I'd completely pissed Dad off.

'And probably for a long time before too,' she decided, making me feel guilty that the half-truths coming from our talk were misleading them when they were trying to understand my recent unhappiness, which must have shown in my behaviour.

51

'**B**ut don't youse see?' I wanted to confess. My guilt at being a secret queer – and therefore a bare-faced liar – swirled within me. 'Dad calls me the retard because I'm a homo! One of *those*!' I ached to shout, with the big voice that everybody knew I had when I was worked up: a declaration that would at least have placed me back in honest communication with the world.

Like I'd felt before Marcus Wright was turned on in the school showers: a time when – even though I was savvy enough to keep the veneers of my eyes steady while my gaze went from lad to lad – I'd *felt* no awareness of the filth within me.

And, in fact, it'd been a curious dialogue with God as I was surrounded by naked lads of my own age at three thirty every Wednesday: a situation in which, although I knew my response wasn't exactly proper, I was untroubled.

Hey up, God! Here we go again! Please God keep my willy soft! Jesus, God! You've given Trevor Carlton such a whopper! Please, God, stop me thinking like that! Blimey! Harton's got balls like a grapefruit! Please, God, have a heart! I can't cope with balls as well as cocks! Strewth! Clarkey's has got a bend in it! Please, God, stop me thinking like that! Bloody hell – Smithy's is nice!

And so it'd continued, week after week, a tingly joy that – although I didn't want to think like *that* – puzzled me by feeling innocent. Apart from which, wasn't it easy to promise God that I was only looking, not *wanting*, like the freaky homos that the games teacher Mr Heston regularly warned us about? Men who hung around public toilets or lured you into bushes, he said, while we stripped off our muddy kit and dived into the communal showers where being naked was so normal that nothing could dirty it. Even if we were constantly interrupted by Mr Heston sticking his hairless pink blob of a head around the tiled entrance to continue his tirade against queers, and – true to another of my impossible promises – I tried not to look at the bottoms.

Especially Trevor Carlton's: his perfect buttocks could've been cut from the lump of marble that the *Gazette* reported was then being made into the statue of Sir Winston Churchill.

'Yup, boys!' our teacher would cry into our warm pink blur. 'Beware public lavatories! Beware bushes! Beware homos! Beware! Beware! Beware!' he climaxed, usually getting me laughing because, by some trick of the light, the centres of his eyes became red, as if he had X-ray vision for peering through steam.

Then Marcus had come out of the showers with his hard willy and Trevor Carlton led the cries of 'Homo!' with Mr Heston – who'd been a naval officer in the war – storming that no boy stooped to queerness on his watch. He emphasized the point by laying three whacks of the cane across Marcus's backside – which, I couldn't help noticing, was nice and that, despite the protection of his trousers (Mr Heston had *screamed* at him to put them on 'immediately'), must have been bruised. Like he was for ever branded the poofter. The nancy. The *queer*.

52

Following all that went wrong for Marcus, the school showers became connected to the shit-stinking public-bog queerness that Mr Heston spoke of.

'Just make me normal,' I instructed God, with whom by day I was well and truly out of patience. And yet whom by night I needed more and more as I was driven increasingly crazy in the head. Even though I was doing my best to stop the willy-watching, in my dreams the classmates who owned those willies brought soft lips to my bed, lovemaking that was tender and joyful until the moment I awoke to sheets whose clagginess impressed my filth upon me. Horrifying sticky queerness that, night after night, spurted out of my *own* body, proving Dad was right to reject me as the vilest of the vile.

'Please, God, don't make me be like Marcus at school,' I begged. The darkness of the room made me feel so small it was as if my terror of a lonely chutney-prodding life to come had also escaped me as I slept and now – encapsulated by the gloom I peered into – was all around me.

Terror that by day was hidden but constant, an inside-my-head darkness that I dared not explore for fear of confronting my death. Like Marcus Wright nearly did when he took his mum's sleeping pills.

Please, God, make me normal. Please, God, make me good. Please, God, make me not be queer like Marcus at school. Please, God, make me dream of girls at night, not boys. Please, God, make me normal. Please, God, make me normal.

Please, God, are you there?

53

Yet the funny thing about my words with God was that we weren't even churchy. It's just that, when we were younger, Dad had encouraged us kids to attend Sunday school, and even used to do the Lord's Prayer with us before we went to bed.

Or, at least, that was what happened until the night he was really drunk and Mum didn't let him reach 'Amen'. She went ape because he'd said, 'Forgive us our treacle' instead of 'Forgive us our trespasses', which, she added, were so many in the case of her lousy husband that the Lord would be on double-time.

Then Dad had really gone off on one, claiming he was married to a heathen with no respect for Higher Spirits, and she'd replied that she had no problem with any Higher Spirit; she merely objected to it being forty per cent proof.

My brother Jack said, 'Amen,' and had us kids giggling so hard that Mum and Dad went quiet and exchanged suspicious looks. It seemed they couldn't decide whether it was him or her who was getting laughed at, and who'd won their godly scrap – though in a way we kids were the losers: Dad never prayed with us again.

But the argument wasn't over: in a later fight about the

loopy things he said when he was plastered, Mum claimed that since he'd asked the Lord to forgive us our treacle, we were the only teenagers on earth who believed that Lyle's Golden Syrup was as biblical as the bread we ate it with.

Dad snorted that if she considered Mother's Pride biblical, she was more of a heathen than he'd thought. She did one of her biggest laughs and suggested a cup of tea. That was how a lot of their fighting went – like they were Tom and Jerry, and got a shock each time the ugly violence came between them. As it always did. Eventually.

54

The silvery light that had earlier foretold the end of the rain had been replaced by sunshine that poured into the kitchen. My brother and sister had just knocked me sideways by announcing that they thought I should stop helping Dad in the workshop.

'I can't do that!' Tears spilled on to my cheeks at the same time as I noted that Picasso was watching us with a dully gleaming eye. 'What if you had to stop your painting?' I demanded of Jack, whose gaze had the strength of rivets.

'And what if you had to stop your flipping wonky dressmaking?' I asked Vanessa, whose eyes flickered with hurt that – despite my anger – shamed me, and made me extra forceful with my final question. 'And what if Rachael had to give up her sports?'

Vanessa retorted that they'd never said I had to give up cars, while Jack – in defiance of the tears that were suddenly in his eyes – pointed out that he wouldn't have suggested coming to the auctions with me if they were trying to stop me loving pink Cortinas. I muttered an apology, accompanied by the squiggle that went down my spine whenever I was reminded that my brother was easily hurt.

Next thing, our sister drew a loud breath and explained

that they'd been concerned about me being in the workshop because, on top of the *protégé*-mentor stuff, Dad's bullying of me had clearly worsened after Jack had stopped him thumping Mum. It seemed so obvious now that I was amazed I hadn't made the connection before.

'So,' I wanted to be sure I'd got it right, 'where he used to clatter Mum, he now whips me?'

'Exactly,' replied Jack, flashing a dead-certain look that went from me to his twin. Then he said Dad had switched 'punchbag for whipping boy'.

'But even if that's true,' I wanted to shout, 'it's unfair because Dad alone knows the filthy secret of what I am!'

But how could I have told them that when queers were so despised by everyone? Jack had informed me that Ted Heath was kicked out as prime minister because he was a shirt-lifter.

55

I promised to *think* about spending less time in the workshop and was relieved that this was enough to bring the smile back to Jack and Vanessa's eyes, which were so full of care that I felt a new wave of fear at losing their love should they discover the truth about me.

Still, there was no way I was going to take sleeping pills like Marcus Wright. Besides, I'd begun to hope that I could earn God's forgiveness for my diseased soul by looking after Mum and Dad, who, at fifty-five, were going to need it when they became infirm (like our grandparents, who'd all popped off when we kids were younger).

So, I had a plan. While my brother and sisters knew which colleges they would eventually go to, I felt I'd already served my time in the workshop with Dad. The proof was the cash I'd got hidden in a marmalade jar at the back of the mahogany wardrobe that spooked me when I woke in the night: six hundred and eleven quid that I'd earned by fixing the bodywork on cars in the streets around ours. It was more than enough to buy five tatty Ford Escorts, or similar, and – after a bit of work – turn at least a hundred quid profit on each: the beginning of my life as a motor trader, who would have a forecourt away from home with a space to the rear for selling the trade-ins I wouldn't have to bother with.

Dad was going to be my sales manager, an important job that he would accept in return for having taught me about cars. He'd shave away his unruly whiskers and swap his buttonless overcoat – and all his other ragged clothes – for a suit. That would be the first thing I'd buy with the business account started with the two grand that was sure to be in the marmalade jar by my sixteenth birthday.

From then on it would be simple. My handsome dad would get his self-respect back and – because he'd have stopped drinking – would be called by his proper name, not Old Boozy, the hopeless staggering drunk. I'd hated the bullies at the car auction for that with all my heart. Then Mum and Dad would be okay together. Hadn't she always said that the man she'd loved enough to marry *twice* was still somewhere inside him? And didn't I *want* them to adore each other again, if only we could stop Dad being so angry?

Which was where I knew I could *really* help: by showing him that, although I had a queer soul, I would never actually become one of *those*. That was the key to putting everything right. I'd succeed with the cars and prove that he hadn't fought in the war just for me to be a filthy stinking homo. That was what I was going to do. Save Dad. Save Mum. Save myself. All of which I swore to God. Who still didn't seem to hear my prayers.

Then again, I'd hardly expected a burning bush in Mum's iris garden, which, at its best, was fantastically colourful and showed the vivacity that pounded in her ocean-going liner of a heart, as Dad put it when he was in a funny mood. It reminded us that he still loved her very much. Even if Jack did quip that the *QE2* was a big ocean-going liner, but had needed a tug to tow her to shore after her propeller broke, leaving her dangerously adrift.

56

Jack's chair fell back and landed with a thump that made Picasso squawk and flap his wings against his cage.

'Sir Wankalot!' cried my brother, crazily lunging for Mum's smelly mop. 'Sir Wankalot yourself!' I retorted, tripping him and moving fast to put my foot on his chest. I had him pinned on the lino as I held the mop over his laughing face.

'Idiots!' protested Vanessa.

'Give a younger brother an inch and he takes a yard!' Jack complained, then turned his face aside so that droplets from the grey strands would miss his mouth – he was laughing too much to close it.

'Silence!' I ordered, giving the mop a jab, which made him clench his lips into a wonky line, reminding me of Vanessa's needlework. When I said as much, she threatened to shove the mop and the galvanized bucket up my bum.

'Just let him scrub my face first!' pleaded Jack, who knew that if she did attack, the mop was certain to make extra forceful contact with him.

'When I'm ready, Sir Wankalotty,' I teased, touching the longest strands to his forehead to see if he would bring an end to it by pulling the mop on to himself.

145

Vanessa's protest that we were upsetting Picasso made me think she'd also anticipated this. 'I mean it! You're really disturbing him!' she insisted, trying not to laugh as we went mad with giggling at our randy parrot, who was busy with his water-butt again.

'Stop!' she screamed, as I gave my brother a jab while his mouth was open. The last time I'd done that he'd had to visit our stuck-up dentist – the one Rachael called Mr Nogood – with inflammation of his gums.

'Say "I am the biggest Sir Wankalot"!' I instructed my brother, leading the battle of the mop towards its usual climax.

'You are the biggest Sir Wankalot!' he defiantly shouted, his shining green eyes like dinner plates.

'Not me, ya fool!' I shoved the stinky grey wetness into his mug. 'You! You're the biggest Sir Wankalot!' I cried triumphantly, while Vanessa wailed that he was going to die of typhoid. I said, no, he wasn't, because the pee on the toilet floor was mostly his anyway.

'I'll get you for this, Craig!' he promised, as I clattered the mop into its bucket and ran to the back door. Beyond it, the sun was bringing steam from the drying concrete around Mum's big green ferns so the yard I passed through on my return to the workshop was like a ghostly forest.

The double-width up-and-over door at the front of the gloomy workshop was fully raised so that the brown Vauxhall Victor Dad had been repairing – and was now parked in the sunny back lane – was like an image on a cinema screen.

'Ah,' said Dad to Big Eddie, who was resting his bum against the side of the car, 'our absentee returns.'

'I'm sorry, Dad,' I began, wary that he was still seething over the wrong-bolt fiasco and liable to blow up in front of my special friend.

'No problem, our Craig,' he said, as calm as Jess Yates on Valium. Then he told me that he didn't want me taking to heart all the things he came out with when he was angry. 'Do you hear me, son?' His eyes were kinder than they'd been in a long time. 'I mean it. It's . . .' he glanced at Big Eddie, who shrugged and smiled at me, '. . . it's the booze that's pickled my brain.'

Then they went for a walk on the seafront.

I feared they were going to discuss me and became so hot I could have burst into flames – except that as my limbs got weak and my mind went fuggy, I was no longer Craig the kid: I was myself again, Brucie the mangy Collie Cross, who had been brought that day to Ginger's house from the kennels.

'C'mon, Brucie-Wucie-Lucie darling!' cried the kid, as my sore and sticky eyes opened. He was crouched at the front of the boiling workshop that'd had the plastic roof fitted by Big Eddie after Raymond's death. 'Drinkies,' he urged, proffering my fish bowl. I struggled on to my legs to lap from it while he cursed himself for leaving me to get too hot while he was welding Big Eddie's red Ford Mustang. 'Sorry,' he whispered, when I'd finished the water.

'I promise I do love you,' he added, looping his arms about me and pressing the side of his face to my neck.

Over his shoulder I saw a familiar figure speeding down the lane on a yellow Raleigh Chopper that gleamed where the sun caught its chrome wheels and *Easy Rider* handlebars.

Why's the kennel lad coming *here*? I wondered, as my mind cleared of its fug.

'What the heck?' cried the kid, as he turned and saw our fast-approaching visitor, whose huge grin, windswept blond hair and reddened face conveyed a spirit that was as free as hope and joy doing a tango in the sky.

'Yahoo!' he called, as I noted happily that his work overalls had been replaced by a sleeveless mustard T-shirt and cut-off dark blue denims. They revealed legs as tanned and muscular as the arms that braced him when he stood on the pedals. I barked a big welcome, my tail wagging for all its worth.

'Yahoo, Ber-rucie!' he responded, as he locked the Chopper's rear brake and laid down a long, curvy skidmark that ended just outside the workshop. Craig's startled cry 'Marcus Wright!' enabled me to make the connection between the kennel lad and the youngster who'd been so bullied at school he'd been driven to take his mum's sleeping pills. I found that *almost* unbelievable: his light blue eyes shone with humour, but he was surrounded by a redness even richer than it had been when I'd known him as the kennel lad. A shade so thrillingly optimistic, it easily matched Ginger's.

'That's me!' he cried, confirming his identity with self-teasing camp, 'The *infamous* Marcus Wright!' He chuckled and used his spine against the backrest to lever the front of the Raleigh Chopper high into the air. It was an amusingly cocky stance that suggested if Craig was brave enough to accept a place on the saddle, then a glorious ride was theirs to be had.

A ride I wanted to happen so much that I did more barking at Marcus. He burst out laughing at the same moment as Craig, their shared delight made even more special when Marcus twisted one of the luminous green grips on the handlebars as if it were an accelerator – except that each growly rev of the engine came from the back of his throat. 'Ber-rucie! Ber-rucie!' he revved, bringing on my seal wiggle as I cleared the couple of yards from the kid to him and licked his free hand where it dangled by the rear wheel. 'Ber-rucie.' He grinned at me before he lowered the front of the bike, shifted to the middle of the saddle and nonchalantly held the handlebars with both hands, one foot to the pedals, the other to the ground.

'Well . . .' he said to Craig, who, to my disappointment, took a backward step into the workshop. 'Here we both are. You and me, Craig. Plus the one and only Brucie-Wucie-Lucie, of course.'

The kid shrugged and smiled, like he fondly regarded himself a fool for giving me such an odd moniker in front of everybody at the kennels. It was a relaxed moment that gave way to new tension: Marcus was staring as if he had something *really* important to say – or maybe just to open up. Instead of asking the kid a proper question, all he said again was 'Well?'

One tiny word that made Craig squirm until I half expected his furry caterpillars to desert him for a worthier host: a notion that made me feel disloyal. I needed to understand his shiftiness, and my second sight opened to numbers chalked on a dusty blackboard in a mathematics room. They were faced by a taller youth, good-looking in a regular sort of way, with wavy black hair that tumbled down each side of his face to where his green and yellow school tie hung in a buckled Y. A young human whose name I'd come to know as Trevor Carlton.

60

'I 'll tell ya what,' said Trevor, keeping his grey eyes on the kid as he took the gum he'd been chewing out of his mouth. 'Ya can slap this in his blond poofter hair. Otherwise', he continued, as Craig reluctantly accepted the sticky wad between his thumb and first finger, 'I'll know you're probably as queer as he is. Won't I?' he asked, glaring at Marcus, then looking back at the kid while making a show of tugging at his own crotch.

'But how can I?' asked Craig, a strawberry blotch even redder than his flushed cheeks spreading over the left side of his neck. 'I mean, I can't just slap gum in somebody's hair,' he added. Panic made his words collide until he bit his lower lip: a family trait, seen particularly in Jack – who really should've had no flesh left to set his teeth against.

Unlike the kid, who now freed his lip and drew a deep breath to steady his nerves before he suggested that, even if they were doing it to a shirt-lifting homo, he'd still be in serious trouble for gumming his hair. That drew an involuntary shudder from Marcus, who'd clearly decided that no reaction was the best response to the attack he was undergoing.

An attack that the kid now attempted to portray as jovial, remarking with forced laughter that, as far as queers went, the one standing with them was an okay person. 'Aren't you, Mandy darling?' he asked Marcus.

Despair at what I was seeing him do made me sink into dark, cold and lonely depths.

'Just do it and rub it in so he has to cut it out,' snapped Trevor, as he moved to block the doorway that Craig had craftily stepped aside to clear for Marcus – who was pale with dread at what was obviously about to happen.

'Because if ya don't,' Trevor continued, as the kid glanced to where other pupils were passing in the corridor, 'no probably about it. It'll *prove* you're the same as he is!'

The hate inside Trevor made his eyes as hard as concrete and his nicely shaped mouth into something nasty that forced me deeper into my depths.

'Do it!' he shrieked, while Craig stared in loathing at the chewed bubble gum that was squidged between his thumb and finger, his brow crinkling in would-be rebellion, his teeth biting so hard on his lower lip that I expected blood.

'Oh, shite,' he said wearily, as he shoved his thumb and finger into Marcus's shining, bouncy hair. Following which, he glumly stood away from his victim, whose eyes firmly rested on Trevor – a young human I should've have hated with a vengeance, yet who now appeared so confused that I pitied him as much as I was in awe of the black all around him.

'Don't be giving *me* the evil eye!' he cried, as Marcus fingered the gum in his hair. 'It was only a joke!' he added, with hysterical giggling that rippled into my freezing darkness until I feared I might drown.

'Well, thanks very much, Trevor,' said Marcus, as he hitched his haversack further on to his shoulder. 'And to you 'n' all,' he told the kid, whose eyes resembled smashed-up dinner plates glued together all wrong. 'Just what I needed,' he concluded, walking tall as he went into the corridor.

'Queer,' spat Trevor to Craig, as he made yet another tug at his own crotch.

61

I surfaced like a bubble from a rusting wreck on the sea bed.

'Yep,' called Marcus to the kid, as my return to the great heat of the workshop sent new shivers through me, 'he's too hot. Far, far too hot,' he added, caressing one of the bigger patches of my surviving hair.

'I know *that*,' responded Craig, who was returning from filling my fish bowl, 'but he's seeing the vet tomorrow. In fact,' he added, with touching pride at his family's speedy care for my wellbeing, 'the very first thing our mum did after coming from the kennels was to book him in for treatment. So there's anything causing it, apart from the sun, it'll be getting sorted along with his mange. Won't it, Brucie darling?' he asked, looking at me through the bowl cupped in his hands. My eyes bulged against their sore lids as I thought I spotted a plump goldfish swimming in my water, its sparkly reddish-gold scales bringing back the joy that had been absent from the depths I'd just been to, depths so *very* scary I prayed never to return to them.

'See how he's staring back at you through the bottom of the glass?' Marcus asked, making my tail do its now pathetic best to wag against the concrete I was lying on. 'That's because he loves you already,' he explained, with an affectionate look that made the kid blush and spill a little of the water as he placed it between my paws. I made them laugh by pricking my ears and doing a double-take, just in case a plump goldfish *was* swimming in the bowl I was about to lap from.

'Drinkies,' said Craig, unable to resist a smile at Marcus as he touched the refreshingly cool water to my dry and itchy nose. 'That's it, darling dog,' he encouraged, lowering his eyes to avoid Marcus's tender gaze. My shivers settled as I lapped. I became aware of their hands resting close on my back and yearned for their fingers to entwine – which was highly unlikely because the kid was terrified of any physical contact that might release his queerness.

Suddenly he got off his haunches and stepped six or seven feet back until he was beside the rear wheel of the Ford Mustang. The car's cherry redness cast a strong glow where the sun was now directly above the clear-topped workshop.

'So,' asked Marcus, as he, too, stood up and looked across the gulf that had opened between them, 'still afraid of me, Craig?'

'Says who?' replied the kid. To my despair, he had so much white around him it was like a shroud, and his smashed-up dinner plates appeared so precarious that I half expected them to fall out in pieces, leaving him in total darkness.

'Nobody,' answered Marcus. Then he calmly explained that Craig was so *obviously* terrified of him that even the man in the moon could have seen it without being told. 'And that being the case,' he continued, licking his finger and drawing a line in the air before his tummy, 'this, Craig, is your imaginary wall against me. Ha! Your very own Berlin Wall,' he added, in a bad German accent that made the kid's brow lift. He stepped forward. 'Clonk!' He grinned broadly.

Craig blanked the humour. 'Clonk,' he told himself. His resignation was matched by my sadness; I'd realized that, on top of his fear, the kid was shocked that – after all the promises of non-queerness he'd made to himself and God – he was in danger of falling in love with somebody who was as queer as they came.

All in all, it was a mess of corrupted emotion that I wanted to take from within him and bury where it could never be dug up, freeing him to embrace the love that would make his life joyful – if only he could find the courage to shake off the self-hate that Raymond and school had burdened him with.

'Be seeing ya,' said Marcus, hardly looking at the kid as he strode out of the workshop to where the gleaming chrome of the yellow Raleigh Chopper briefly blinded me. 'So long, Brucie,' he called, swinging his leg over the saddle and rocking the bike from its stand.

I cursed myself as a useless romantic mongrel.

62

But the kid strode forward to where the tips of his brogues stuck over the small ramp at the edge of the workshop. 'Don't go!' he cried.

Rather than cycling away, as he'd been set to do, Marcus took his foot from the pedals and began scuffing the heel of his plimsoll on the long, curvy skidmark that he'd made earlier. 'Why?' he asked, seemingly intrigued by the ease with which he was creating a gap in the black strip

Before Craig could answer, my second sight opened to where he was with Trevor Carlton and other boys in varying states of undress, all of whom were watching Marcus get caned by their red-faced PE teacher, who furiously shouted that no boy was allowed to stoop to queerness on his watch. Words that made me want to bite. Not least because each time he delivered a lash, Mr Heston failed to discourage the onlookers from jeering, as if poor Marcus had somehow committed a personal crime against each of them and therefore deserved nothing less than mob hatred.

The kid was shrouded by a deathly black that equalled Trevor's, a grim fact that made my heart race until each beat smashed into the next. Mercifully, I didn't actually collapse in the hot air of the lane outside the workshop, where

Marcus was again twisting one of the luminous green handlebar grips as if it were an accelerator.

'Why, Craig? Why do you *want* me to stay?' he persisted.

My fury with Mr Heston was rapidly waning as I yearned for the kid to answer with more than just words.

Kiss him!

Hug him!

Touch him!

Love him!

I barked and barked as I ran in circles around the Raleigh Chopper, an episode during which, for dizzying seconds, I was *within Craig's eyes* in the horrid changing rooms, and somehow within the eyes of the other boys too, slithering this way and that as I peered around corners. All to be sure that nobody was seeing that I too deserved a caning for being queer.

Except, of course, this had happened months earlier and now Marcus was laughing at my barking while standing with the Raleigh Chopper's low crossbar resting between his legs. 'That barmy bloody dog!' he exclaimed, as Craig came into the lane to give me affection that made me rear up and rest my paws on his shoulders. His green eyes were wide with joy as my long pink tongue met his nose. I got a bitter taste of burned under-body sealant from the welding on Big Eddie's car.

'Ya see, Craig!' continued Marcus. 'Brucie doesn't *just* love you, he adores you to bits! Just look at him!' he cried, clapping his hands as I did my best to lick Craig's cheeks and brow so that the sun could soothe his skin without welding filth being in the way.

Craig, love Marcus!
Marcus, love Craig!

I barked and barked and leaped and leaped, my delight growing even greater as Marcus cycled around us, declaring that I was leaping so high because the offal I'd been fed at the kennels was kangaroo brain.

'But he doesn't eat kangaroo!' the kid gaily responded. 'Do you, Brucie-Wucie?' he asked, kissing my nose, then lowering me to the ground, where I lay exhausted across a dip that was for channelling rainwater in the centre of the lane.

'Maybe not,' responded Marcus, looking down at the crouched kid as he braked to a halt with a mini-skid. 'But', he pointed out, 'you still haven't said why you want me to stay. Have you?' he asked.

Craig rested a hand on my side and inhaled deeply as he collected his thoughts.

I held my breath in anticipation of what he would say.

63

Sickly sweetness filled my mouth as my runaway second sight opened again, this time briefly to reveal the bubble gum in Marcus's hair. To my relief, Craig let go of the breath he'd been holding – any more of that malarkey and I might have died in the lane that separated Ginger's house from the Heartbreak Hotel.

'I wanted to say sorry,' he began, his eyes no longer dinner plates, but as winningly intense as Jack's and Vanessa's were whenever they were trying to get information out of him. 'I'm really, really sorry.' Marcus met his eyes and raised his left foot to the crossbar of the Raleigh Chopper, then slipped a finger into his plimsoll to scratch his instep, which was what I needed to do to my itchiest area. It was slightly beyond my reach, where my first human always touched the electric cable to my spine.

'Sorry for what?' asked Marcus, leaving his foot on the crossbar as he took his finger out of the plimsoll and locked his rear brake. 'For laughing when I was beaten by Mr Heston?'

Craig winced as if he was being caned now.

'Or', he continued, 'for joining in with those who spat on me and shoved me about every day for weeks? Like *they* were ever *your* friends, Craig.'

The kid was crimson. Marcus returned his foot to the ground and slid backwards on the long, thin saddle to lever the front of the Raleigh Chopper into the air again.

'Yes!' Craig blurted, as if an obstinate tooth had been pulled from his gum. 'For all that stuff I'm truly sorry,' he continued, stepping nearer to Marcus, who looked down and smiled at me, as if it was important that even a mangy Collie Cross should understand that he intended no harm towards the kid.

'So,' he looked at Craig with calm eyes, 'that's it, then? You're sorry and everything's forgotten? Simple, really, isn't it?' he asked, but more of himself than Craig, as he raised the front of the shiny yellow bike even higher into the air.

'Do ya reckon?' retorted the kid, who now sagged with such despair that Marcus frowned and lowered his wheel back to the concrete.

'Look,' he began, trying to fix Craig's guilty eyes, which were as slippery as eels, 'none of it was your fault. So do yourself a favour and forget it.' His hands tightened around the luminous green handlebar grips as his right foot found its natural place on the pedal: preparations for departure that – although my legs were so weak I could've been returned to Psycho Vet under the Trades Description Act – drove me to stand firm between him and the kid, who was biting his lower lip as if he hadn't been fed for a year.

'But I can't just *forget* it!' he said, with a vehemence that drove the slipperiness from his eyes. 'I'm way too ashamed! Especially about the gum!' The self-hate that was over-whelming him made every millimetre of my already itchy skin feel as if maggots teemed beneath its scabby surface. It was a sickening reminder of my own worthlessness; I was ashamed for believing *I* was the one to help Craig. Marcus advised him to calm down.

I took the weight off my increasingly wobbly legs by squatting on my bum. I drew comfort from where my side rested against Marcus's solid calf muscle, making us a joint force whose purpose was to help Craig discover the joy that was rightfully his. My eyes hurt as I gave him the widest look I could possibly muster.

'Brucie-Bruce,' he murmured, in imitation of Big Eddie's way of saying my name, his car-mucky fingers touching my dry nose before he lifted his gaze back to Marcus and repeated that, above all, he regretted the gum. 'Truly,' he insisted.

Marcus shrugged off the attack as though it wasn't such a big deal when any mutt worth its keep would have known that Marcus would remember it for the rest of his life. 'Forget it, Craigie.' He laughed with such warmth that my heart felt as though liquid gold was passing through it. 'It doesn't matter,' he insisted, as I showed my growing love for him with another lick of his hand where it rested on his thigh.

From the puzzlement I could see in the kid's eyes, I knew the conversation wasn't over yet.

64

Craig moved so close that my head was squashed between his smelly work jeans and Marcus's leg – its hardness reminded me of my first human's favourite television programme – *The Incredible Hulk*.

'But you tried to kill yourself! Everybody knows! You took your mum's pills!' he cried, sending hot and cold waves through me as images of the muscly Hulk were replaced with a disturbing vision of Marcus filling his belly with capsules taken from a dark brown medicine bottle.

'So that's what they whisper about me, is it?' he asked, his thigh twitching against my head as if he was being given an electric shock now.

'But you bloody did, Marcus!' protested Craig. He stepped back, freeing me.

'*Please* don't say important things don't matter,' he added.

Marcus sighed and rested his forehead where his right arm made a bridge to the front of the bike. 'Okay,' he agreed, as he locked both brakes and jabbed the handlebars. The front tyre bulged against the ground. 'Okay!' he cried, four more times to four more jabs and four more bulges, each movement less violent than the one before. 'Okay, *Mister* Craig!' He faced the kid with a burst of laughter that made me happier for them both – even if Craig was now so sadly unresponsive that I had to resist the urge to do my kiss-him-hug-him-*love*-him routine. Because that was me in those early times. Never wanting the difficult stuff to happen. Even when it was as necessary as a life-saving operation.

Yet it wasn't about me, was it? It was about them. And when Marcus realized Craig's desolate state, he put his spine to the backrest and levelled his head so that he was facing up the lane in the direction he'd come from. 'Know what I really think?' he asked, without looking at Craig. 'Ya right. There's no point denying it. I *did* try to do myself in with my mum's pills.' He closed his eyes so that his long gold-blond lashes became extra thick lines – they were like the serried ranks of wires on the brush my first human used on his shoes before going out in his teddy-boy suit.

'And yes, again,' he continued. 'I would've succeeded if it wasn't for my dad coming home poorly from work and shoving my head down the bog, which – just my luck – wasn't even clean. And, yes, yes, yes, it *was* because of the bubble gum and Trevor Carlton and Mr Heston and all the stuff people say about the likes of us.' Craig sucked in a loud breath. 'Or', he corrected himself, as he opened his eyes, 'the likes of *me*, not you, matey.'

He set his other foot on the crossbar to scratch his foot again, once more reminding me that I could never reach my own itchiest bit.

'The likes of me!' he exclaimed, with mock-horror that tricked a grin out of the kid who – for one beautiful moment

– looked as if he might step forward and take his place on the saddle.

Instead he kept his distance, but his voice was gentle even though it was accompanied by another invasion of eels into his eyes. 'Marcus, you're something else *entirely*.'

'Really?'

'You are. A one-off.' His eyes became fixed on the concrete floor. (Big Eddie must've cleaned it after Raymond's death: the layer of oil that had helped make the place so dark was gone.)

'Thanks, Craig,' said Marcus, and gave me a look that got me thinking he *knew* I was willing Craig to lift his gaze from the ground.

Then Marcus lifted his face to the sun and yet again closed his eyes, his right hand slowly twisting the handlebar grip.

Look up and tell him you love him, I willed Craig, as I became dizzied by the red that glowed from Big Eddie's car in the brightness of the sun.

But I now accepted that, whatever lonely depths he'd known as the retard, there were other places the kid needed to sink to before he could enjoy the intimacy his soul craved.

Tell him you love him, I tried once more, but I knew it was hopeless.

65

I believed that Big Eddie could help the kid get free of his self-hate, so when we heard a familiar voice singing 'Are You Lonesome Tonight?', hope returned to me, even before the sneck on the dark green gate clicked and he came into the lane. The sun's glare made his gold jewellery, turquoise shirt and black quiff shine so brilliantly that I had to half close my eyes. To be fair to Elvis Presley – who was getting slammed in the press for becoming as fat as an old Labrador – there'd been no reports of him coming onstage with a monster bacon sandwich like the one on the plate gripped in Big Eddie's right hand.

'Here, Craig lad!' he boomed, as he made his weighty, lop-sided way across the lane. 'Best Danish from Viv! Eat it while it's hot,' he added. He cast an amused glance to the young human on the shiny Raleigh Chopper, who was looking at him quizzically.

'Thanks, Big E,' muttered the kid. The return of the strawberry blotch on his neck betrayed his terror that his huge friend would make a connection between himself and the queerness of Marcus, who now cleared his throat so loudly that Craig was jolted into returning his gaze.

'Did I tell you I'm going to live in London?' Marcus asked.

The kid was stunned. I followed his troubled eyes to the watchful face of Big Eddie – whose memories and interior voice were now abruptly *mine*. It was a sudden and powerful move by my second sight and I feared that, before I could return to being *me*, I'd have the heart attack that'd got Big Eddie's number written on it. In case that sounds dramatic, it was generally accepted that if he wanted to make old bones, Big Eddie needed to lose four stones of fat.

But the fear was gone as quickly as it had come, and my focus was where I wanted it to be. Because that was what I'd promised Raymond shortly before his death: that I – Big Eddie Clarkson – would always look out for his younger son: Craig lad.

66

I met Vivienne when we were teenagers and now her ill-health had me so scared of being left alone that I wouldn't have traded an extra moment with her for all the gold bullion in the world. The irony was that her love made me believe in myself as a man. So, when Raymond from across the back lane asked if I believed love between men was wrong, my reply had come readily. Love was all that mattered for us all.

Since I knew he was asking about the nature of young Craig, I added that all four of his children had loving natures and would surely bring happiness to themselves and others.

I spoke sense, he decided, making me ashamed of my behaviour of an hour before when, from the backyard at my hotel, I'd heard him bawling at Craig like he was a madman. Hard, hard words that'd boiled my blood until I'd wanted to shake him and ask what on God's earth he was doing, hammering at a youngster who you could see worshipped him. And who – above all – needed his approval. His love.

I'd waited in the rain, all the while spying from a knot-hole in the back gate, determined, against my wife's wishes, to tackle Raymond when the laddie was out of the way. As it happened, that came about when Jack called for him to go inside.

Raymond was working on an old brown Vauxhall. Given the combination of my height and the fact that he was squatting where the back wheel was off, I towered over him as I promised that if I ever heard him bullying the youngster again I'd punch his lights out. I was braced for anger but received a weary sigh and a nod of understanding that suggested he was relieved *somebody* was at last willing to put the brakes on his fury with his son.

'Help me finish this damn thing, Eddie,' he said, meaning the suspension assembly on the Vauxhall. So there we were for the next hour. No reference to how I'd also told him that he was a gutless yellow-bellied coward who, if not punching his wife, was hurting his children. Just a quiet companionability as his fingers became more nimble and the sun did away with the rain that'd helped turn the garage into a sodden Hell that would've tested Mother Teresa. By the time Craig returned, the Vauxhall was up and running and the lane was all steamy where the sun was changing the mood of the day.

'Walk with me,' suggested Raymond, and set off towards the sea, which had turned from a dark grey to a shiny blue that underlined one surprising thing. No matter how violent he was with his fists or his tongue, I couldn't – I simply *couldn't* – judge this troubled man.

'Sure I'll walk with you,' I said, as curious as I was moved that he appeared to have faith in me.

67

I see three on the promontory that day. First, the round-bellied figure of Sir Winston Churchill, his back ramrod straight as he looks across the sea from where he stands high on his plinth of circular stone steps. His white marble body sparkles.

Then there's me sitting on the seaward bench below the statue, my quiff destroyed by the rain.

And finally there's a heavily bearded man, who's lost in his thoughts as he rests his left hand on the railing while staring out to sea, his right fingers holding a cigarette, his oily red jumper made comical by the bits of white shirt that stick out of its holey elbows. His feet are protected by black wellingtons, cut down to ankle-height.

'You'll have to let me know where you got the boots, Raymond,' I said, to break the tricky silence that'd marked our walk from the lane. 'Could do with some of those,' I added. 'No offence.'

He flicked his cigarette aside, turned to me and enquired if I could imagine the ocean on fire.

'No,' I replied, my gaze held fast by his steel-blue eyes as he drew his hand up the whiskery side of his face and through his wild grey hair. His head tilted back so that I saw yellowed teeth as he appeared to offer a silent prayer to Sir Winston.

'Ah!' he said, lowering his eyes back to me. 'It's only us who were there that have the damnable *imagining* of it. Only us who were there.'

68

'After the hit of the torpedo comes the clamour that sees you jumping overboard and thrashing for your life while your skin is scorched by flames, twenty, thirty, maybe forty feet high. Immense mountains of fire that constantly change shape above your pathetic little human head, with evil-smelling smoke so thick and black that day is now night.

'An unnatural darkness where your fear of immolation plays against the loud wrenching of your ship as it upends and slides under, its deathly moans reverberating against your lower body as it goes down, all the while bleeding diesel that feeds the *abomination* of an ocean, which, against all the laws of nature, against all the laws of God, is now an even greater inferno.

'Fiercely hot yellow, orange and red flames that roar like the devil's breath and have the swell of the waves, through which – by sheer luck – you're borne this way and that, with all the damn oil you've swallowed making you want to vomit your insides up.

'And then you're assailed by another terror, one from within your own stupefied mind: a strong, strong – *dangerously strong* – inclination to give up and swim into the heart of it, where men, *boys* in their early twenties and younger, whom you've known like family, scream for their mothers as they cook like lobsters in a pan. Their agonized faces, which you glimpse here and there through the fire, are literally melting to the bone. Crewmates, whose hideous deaths sear your mind so that you never stop feeling guilty that you – *you* – were a so-called lucky one who floated untouched.'

69

Raymond's aloneness made me slide my hands beneath my thighs on the bench, as if this simple action would prevent me talking when it was clear no words could match what I'd just heard – at least, not unless I'd been there when the ocean was ablaze, and was therefore part of an exclusive group with a *right* to discuss it.

With an appreciative nod, he turned back to the horizon and lit another cigarette. The smoke that was soon swirling around his shaggy outline reached my nostrils and stirred a need in me to speak of a horror I most certainly *did* comprehend: Vivienne's lung cancer and the loss I would soon be facing. But, just as strongly as I understood that Raymond was not yet through with his confessional, I felt it would be wrong for me to compete with him in the pain stakes.

For which reason I also kept to myself the memory of a young father who was killed at Dunkirk when I – his only child – was still in short pants, and also the story of my mother, who upon her death when I was in my mid-thirties, was convinced that the attending male nurse was the love of her life back from where he'd been fighting in France.

Such was the war and how it had affected us all, I thought, as I sat with my hands beneath my thighs on the bench beneath Sir Winston, whose gravelly drawl made me smile as I recalled a young laddie pressing his ear to his mother's parlour door to listen to a speech about fighting on the beaches. I was puzzled that we were to resist the Germans in our breeches.

70

I looked to Raymond's right and watched a few gulls swooping and soaring, their freedom to be nothing but themselves as readily expressed by their ear-splitting squawks as it was by the flashes of their diamond white undersides when they rose on high.

'Noisy damn beasts,' said Raymond, who was watching me now. 'In fact,' he continued, as he raised the Denis Healey eyebrows he'd passed on to his children, 'they're despised by many as vermin.'

'Ah,' I said. '"Despised" is a strong word.'

'I suppose it is,' he agreed, his eyes sliding to where he crushed his cigarette end beneath his boot. His head snapped up again, and that was when he popped his question about the rightness of love between men.

My concern for young Craig made me straighten my back and hold my head high – as if that could defend the lad against his father's bullying. Raymond's lips widened and the yellowish skin around his eyes crinkled; for a moment, I feared an explosion, but it was the start of a huge grin, the only occasion when I saw him beam with fatherly pride.

'Eddie, my friend,' he came and sat beside me, 'you may look like an *Opportunity Knocks* reject, but you talk a great deal of sense.'

I laughed at being teased for my appearance by a man who was scruffier than your average tramp, but I was glad that I seemed to have said the right thing. 'Whatever you say, Raymond lad,' I responded, trying to sound casual, when in reality our words had been as loaded as the silence that now hung between us.

A silence that I was careful not to break as I fixed my eyes on the distant meeting of the darker blue sea with the paler blue sky, a line so neat it might've been painted by God's hand.

'I want you to do something for me,' he announced, his voice cracking. The gulls were now flying off with their claws swept back.

'I'm listening,' I said, softening my voice as best I could while gripping a slat of the bench beneath my thighs with both hands, as if otherwise I might have tumbled into the blue that was spread before us.

71

'I want you always to look out for my second son,' he said.

It was a request that made me think two things. One, he was a brave man who, in order to protect his wife and children from his own chaos, was preparing to leave them; and two, that being invited to care for young Craig was the best thing that'd happened to me, apart from marrying Vivienne. Ever since he'd first caught my attention by using Vim, Brasso and a ton of elbow grease to put the shine back on a seriously dull Ford Cortina, I'd been as smitten by the lad's passion for cars as I was concerned by Raymond's attitude towards him. I'd quietly added a couple of hundred pounds to an old mate's offer for what he called the pink projectile: it was worth every penny when the lad's pride at making a sale of six hundred and eighty-five pounds had him walking ten feet tall – which meant I escaped the ear-bashing I would otherwise have copped for being a spendthrift.

To be fair to my wife, she, too, was so taken by the liveliness of the family across the lane that hardly a day passed without a report on which one she'd seen doing what. Her deepest laugh came after she'd got herself settled

179

by the kitchen door to the yard, the cigarette smoke that was so much a part of all that I cherished about her chuffing from her nose and mouth, the tender lips I only had to think of to hurt *physically* at the notion that, sooner rather than later, they would not be there for me to kiss.

'Well, Eddie, I saw Vanessa in the town centre wearing a blouse made from a tablecloth!'

'Well, Eddie, Rachael was at the bus station with a trampolining trophy as big as bucket!'

'Well, Edwin' – I must have been in her bad books – 'young Jack's in the paper for winning a painting competition!'

Such was the nature of her constant reporting. Such, in fact, was our mutual infatuation with all the family across the lane.

72

A policeman who was known, apparently, as Bill the Copper brought the news that, after getting drunk at the Gay Hussar, Raymond was seen by a motorist – who at first thought he was a streaker – to remove his clothes, salute Sir Winston and climb over the sea rail.

Knocked sideways by the suddenness of this turn of events – it happened only hours after our talk – I can't claim I was surprised. I'd already reached the conclusion that here was a man who'd struggled in a particularly cruel sea for a *very* long time.

And while my heart and Vivienne's went out to all his young 'uns – and to their mother, of course – I have to say it was the older lad, Jack, who made the greatest impression when he called for the vicar to delay the sending off of his father: his young face set as he stepped up to kiss the coffin lid, say, 'Goodbye, Dad,' and press the away button himself.

Then he returned to his sister, Vanessa, whose grief – in my wife's surprisingly blunt words – made her look as if a fist had been punched into the middle of her brain. Not that Rachael, Craig or even Jack appeared much better, but where the younger twins had withdrawn into themselves, their older brother was already looking out for at least one of them.

'Hey, Big Man,' he said, his eyes locking with mine as I came out of the crematorium. 'I reckon our kid would love to fix up that rusty old American car of yours.'

At that, the things that had been turning in my mind about Raymond and my promise to look out for young Craig were spinning as fast as a fruit-machine. 'Happen he would, young Jack,' I agreed, and left the lad to shake the hand of the next mourner.

73

We went to America after our wedding in 1955. I was a welder in the Texas oil business and Vivienne was a high-school secretary. With a bit of jiggling on my behalf, we always had the summer to explore the States. For two years we drove around in a clapped-out pre-war Chevy, then bought a blue and yellow Ford Edsel, an immense car of the late fifties that – because of its skinny upright radiator grille – was known as the Ford Ethel.

After ten years we had enough cash to come home and buy a B&B. Our acceptance of childlessness made our marriage even stronger that it already was. I was happy. Vivienne was happy. As proof of our buccaneering years, we were the still fairly young couple who flashed around town in a red Ford Mustang, a car that real-life speed fanatic Steve McQueen had made iconic in *Bullitt*, the film we'd been to see the night my fingertips turned to iron as they happened upon a lump in the lower curve of Vivienne's right breast. Its removal came as swiftly as her consultant's follow-up promise that they'd 'got it all'.

That same year, 1969, one Mr Elvis Presley, whose 1950s rock-and-roll had meant nothing to me, staged his mighty comeback as a singer of ballads about love. His voice smoothed away my fear of losing the person I loved so much that thoughts of life without her brought with them an unbearable darkness. It was somewhere I absolutely did not want to be. Somewhere I absolutely could *not* be.

Two years later we underwent the whole trial again when part of her lower bowel was removed: bad luck but not secondaries, explained another consultant, who added that maybe it was time for Vivienne to stop smoking, a warning she laughed off with a quip: he obviously thought she smoked through her bum.

Elvis had a new loneliness in his voice as he sang of a love that was always on his mind, and somehow it felt right for us to sell the B&B and open our own Heartbreak Hotel. The only thing that spoiled the image we worked so hard to create was the rust that seven British winters had given our Ford Mustang. Neither of us could bear to part with it, and it still looked a million dollars, parked on the forecourt beneath our neon Elvis in his glittering 1973 Hawaii jumpsuit.

We were fine again. We were great again. Until the day not so long ago when Vivienne had a coughing fit. Afterwards the tea-towel I'd given her as a makeshift hanky was bright red with blood.

Now I had everything planned with jackpot certainty before we were even out of the crematorium grounds. First, young Craig and I were going to rip the sodden roof off the workshop and replace it with something that would keep the rain out but allow the light to flood in. Then we'd clean away the oil that'd been compressed into a black carpet that made your feet stick to the ground.

Then we'd do the tatty old brick walls in white, completing the transformation of a depressing cave into a cheery place where I'd teach the young 'un how to gas weld: a skill I'd been so proud of when I was younger that many Texan pipelines had my flowing signature welded to them.

'If he can cut out the rot and let in new steel, he'll be a proper car restorer,' I said, with such enthusiasm that Vivienne told me to be quiet in case I seemed disrespectful to Raymond's memory. I'd forgotten Craig's father as soon as I'd locked on to the idea that, with the lad doing the repairs, the condition of our Ford Mustang would not be terminal after all.

It was a renewal of hope that had me seeing a future in which Vivienne, myself and the laddie would be together in our iconic car that had been cured of its rot: a dream, if you like, that everything would be okay after all.

The kid's voice brought me abruptly back to the workshop. 'Tell me he's not having a heart attack!' he was crying, his furry caterpillars pulled tight over his frantic eyes as he crouched opposite where Big Eddie was kneeling with one hand supporting my underside and the other bracing my spine. Although I was on all four paws, I was not taking my own weight.

'No, laddie, ya new dog isn't having a ruddy heart attack.' He chuckled while shaking me like a toy he was testing for rattles after it'd been dropped. Ironically, my latest bout of the shivers had been caused by my discovery of *his* terror at the prospect of losing his wife.

'Are you sure?' asked the kid, as I was tentatively released to see if my legs were strong enough. When he saw that they were, Big Eddie concluded that – as *everybody* was saying – the day was too hot for me. Especially since I was yet to be treated for my ailments.

'You mean we're neglecting him?' Craig shot a troubled look to where Marcus was still sitting on his Raleigh chopper. Its shine tested my eyes even more than it had earlier.

'*Noooo*, laddie,' said Big Eddie, lengthening the tiny word as he came off his knee before taking several backward steps down the lane to become an onlooker of me, Craig and Marcus, who now took his right foot off the pedal and returned it again. He repeated the move several times before he reminded the kid that he'd said he was going away to London. 'To *live*,' he stressed, staring hard at Craig, whose response was to lower his eyes to the ground and draw my head against his chest, his left hand caressing my under-neck, his right fingers tickling between my ears.

'Why?' he asked eventually, releasing me and standing to face Marcus, who shrugged and looked sad.

'Tell me!' insisted the kid, with a stamp of his foot that made Big Eddie cluck his tongue.

His face brightened when Marcus launched into a reply that put the thrilling redness back into the air around him. 'To study dance! Just like I've always wanted! Me! I mean *me*, Craig! *I'm* going to London to study contemporary dance!'

Craig slunk deeper into the workshop where, despite his naturally olive skin and lovely summer tan, he managed to go so pale that I nearly growled. Big Eddie got in first by urging him to congratulate Marcus, who, in the face of no words from the surly-seeming kid, began riding circles in the lane, his eyes searching for Craig less and less frequently until finally he stood on the pedals for the uphill slog back the way he'd come.

'Ta-ra, Craig! Ta-ra, Mr Heartbreak Hotel! Ta-ra, Brucie-Wucie-Lucie!' he called, making a wiggling seal out of me as I went to the side of the kid, who now looked as though *he*'d had a fist smashed into the middle of his brain.

ig Eddie looked down thoughtfully to where he'd
placed his toe on the long curvy skidmark left by the
Raleigh Chopper and commented that Marcus was
a nice lad who'd make a good friend for Craig –
encouragement that was so kind in its lack of force that I let
out a yap, which made him smile and reassure the kid that
he'd got the best dog in the world and, not to worry, I'd be
fine once the vet had seen me.

Then he was gone through the green gate to Heartbreak
Hotel and I was extra grateful that he didn't sing 'Are You
Lonesome Tonight?' as he went up the yard, not because the
kid looked lonesome but because my thoughts were straying
to when three other tiny pups and I were tied into a sack and
thrown into a river. I was at the top as they drowned.

A horrible event that ended with the chance passing of
my first human, who waded in and massaged me until I was
breathing properly again. The light of the sky after the
darkness I'd just experienced blinded me for the weeks that
I was tended with care, which made me believe the prints
of his fingers had been laid down by acts of love.

So, it was even harder when he first came with a special
electric cable that had a plug at one end and bare wires at
the other. I needed punishing, he said. For what? I'm *still*
wondering.

77

My memory of the remainder of that first day of my new life is fragmented. But I am clear that while the kid tidied the workshop I was in the kitchen, where Ginger knelt on the seahorse lino and applied more of the pinky lotion to my inflamed skin. Then she lifted my chin with her thumb and gazed at me with the big green eyes that were so like all the kids'.

'Well now, Brucie. Is my mad brood going to be okay?' she asked, her bony features softened with amusement that *I* was now her confidant, a position of which I was so proud that I was licking her chin, her mouth, her cheeks, and – the easiest bit – her lovely big battered nose. 'You're a daft animal!' she said, as she stood up, then sat on one of the breakfast chairs. I placed my chin on her lap and felt her hands caressing my neck. My heart was pulsing with the warm gold I've told you about, and my second sight was as incapable of opening to her as it had been with my first human – though, in truth, I was so wearied by all I'd discovered that a break in my investigations was welcome.

'Oh, you lovely, lovely dog!' she cried.

I shuffled my bum forward so that I was as close as I could get without actually climbing up. My head was spinning with impressions of the workshop, the iris garden, the Liquorice Allsort door, the magic forest of ferns, and everything else that she'd put into a home where the kids were free to be creative. Rachael the sporty one, Craig the car nut, Vanessa the clothes designer and Jack the artist: youngsters gifted with the spirit of Ginger, whom I loved more than a mangy mutt had ever loved a human before.

'That bloody Vanessa, Brucie,' she confided, with a smile, as she bent forward to plant a kiss between my eyes. 'She's made my velvet curtain into one her outfits!'

'That bloody Vanessa!' mimicked Picasso. She laughed so hard that I hauled my wobbly bones on to her lap after all.

'Oh, you lovely, lovely dog!' she cried again, hugging me tight and sobbing into my patchy fur.

Not much later – when it was time for tea – I got myself tucked under the table with the feet of the kids all around me. Their conversation took a course that means I can repeat what I did earlier in this story: give the basics and never mind who said what. Because, like all their exchanges, this was merely a skirmish in a war of wits that nobody could have won outright.

'Brucie's sleeping on my bed tonight.'

'He is not. He's sleeping on mine. I've got the biggest bed.'

'Only because you're the fattest.'

'Get stuffed, you!'

'And stop squiggling about, our Rachael!'

'Yes, you'll kick Brucie under the table.'

'I will not!'

'You will! You've got clumsy feet for an athlete.'

'Well, that's better than a clumsy brain!'

'Or no brain at all!'

'Drop dead, Jack!'

'Drop dead yourself, Wankalot!'

'Shut up, our Craig!'

'Yes. The both of you. Shut up right now. You'll upset poor Brucie.'

'You mean *you* will, with a face like that. Lady bloody Gargoyle.'

'Huh! Have you looked in a mirror lately?'

'I'd have a tough job with you always preening!'

'Ah! You see—'

'There you two go again.'

'Oh, so *grown-up* and always fighting like five-year-olds.'

'All the more reason for Brucie to sleep on *my* bed, not theirs. Mum, tell them Brucie's been in the workshop and knows me best.'

'Oh, put a sock in it, our Craig!'

Ginger was barely started on what would have been a full nuclear blast when she was cut off by their gleeful chorus: 'If you bloody kids don't stop fighting right now, Brucie's going back to the kennels! You kids, you bloody cheeky kids!' She was miffed but unable to stop herself joining their laughter. Then she caused further hilarity: when she'd booked me at the vet, she'd encountered Mr Nosgood the dentist, who'd had the teeth of his Pekinese cleaned; a teenage girl, who was getting a white rabbit vaccinated, said she was surprised he hadn't done it on the NHS. A joke that stung Nogood, said Ginger, because patients far and wide were realizing that he did anything to wring money out of the system.

And although I've never had what you'd call a feet fetish

(unlike mutts that enjoy *toes*), on that particular occasion beneath the table, I revelled in the fact that Jack's shoes were smudged with smelly oil paint, that Rachael's plimsolls ponged of her exercises, that Craig's scuffed brogues leaked a sour whiff of unchanged sock and, above all, that Vanessa had swapped her knockabout footwear for shiny custard yellow stilettos, on which she'd painted bright red lady-birds.

Still, the last laugh was Ginger's. When everybody went to the front room to watch a repeat of *The Man from U.N.C.L.E.*, and the crafty kids descended on the broken-backed sofa as one, she coolly ignored their astonishment that its frame held. Like, occasionally she knew things they didn't.

In the event, a bed of coats was made for me in Ginger's bedroom: the one with the upper bay window, from which Rachael had warned that Bill the Copper was coming up the street after Raymond had punched Ginger and was about to get whopped by Jack in the iris garden.

Very soon, of course, I was on the soft double bed, first at the end, then in the middle and finally at the top, where Ginger called me a bad dog and rested her hand on my side. Her light touch, her snoring, and even the darkness of the room were so relaxing that, after I'd gone into a deep sleep, my second sight at last opened to her.

78

A man who was little, round and totally bald had one eye closed and the other pressed to a camera that was on a tripod in a studio where framed photographs of smiling young couples – in which all the men wore military uniforms – were displayed on the walls.

'And . . . just . . . one . . . more . . .' he said, stretching his words as I closed my painful eyes against the flash that accompanied the click of the shutter.

He moved aside discreetly to check his diary while young Raymond planted kisses on the neck of beautiful young Ginger, who'd nuzzled into him and whispered that he'd better not get himself wounded or killed when he went off to war in the smart Navy outfit he was wearing for their photo.

He kissed her again and again, now on her cheeks and lips, with exquisite tenderness, which gave off a redness that, in being a natural blend with her own shade, made me feel great sorrow and even *love* for him.

'*Me*, Missus Wife?' he teased, caressing her shiny auburn hair while meeting her tearful gaze with his own clear blue eyes. 'I'll be your unsinkable sailor!'

And then the man who had snapped the treasured photograph of Ginger and Raymond that, more than thirty years later, had pride of place on the mantel at my new home cleared his throat to advise that the prints would not be available until the following week.

Ginger's explanation that she would return to the studio alone because her husband was sailing the next day killed the sparkle in his hazel eyes: he could no longer pretend indifference to the misery that lay behind the smiles of the young couples in the photographs on the walls around him.

All in all, it was a gloomy situation that led Raymond to quip that since *somebody* had to sort out Hitler's murdering mob it might as well be himself. Ginger declared undying love for her brave 'Mister Husband', who – with a simplicity that touched the innermost part of my soul – retorted that her devotion was just as well, as his feelings for her were greater than the value he placed on life itself.

It was a truly loving exchange that made the photographer – who was about fifty, with a lonely non-colour like Craig's – let out a sob that was barely disguised as cough. Ginger and Raymond turned to him.

'How about . . .' he began, a smile lighting his oddly boyish face as he found a way out of his embarrassment, '. . . how about if about if I frame the last photograph of you delightful young people at no charge?'

'Thank you!' chimed Raymond and Ginger, whose joy made him clasp his perfectly manicured hands together, as if he was satisfied that he'd softened whatever horrors the war had in store for them.

'My pleasure, I'm sure!' He was jiggling his spine as if somebody was walking on his grave.

79

Yet it was me, Brucie, whose life I feared for. Because, as I said earlier, all we mutts know that it's dangerous to use your second sight unless you're fit and well – and what had I done all day but follow my enquiries while I was getting hotter and weaker? The result was almost complete exhaustion, which meant I had no choice but to accept whatever happened next.

That was a visit to the promontory, where Raymond – who was very drunk from the Gay Hussar – set his back to the sea rail, lit a cigarette and looked up at Sir Winston. The white marble face had a faint blush where the declining sun was reflected by the flat, silvery-pink sea.

'You!' he barked. 'You sent me away to that damnably cold Atlantic where five times we were sunk in four years. Ha! But I found comfort – if that was such a mighty crime. A tiny fair-haired pup of a thing. The same age as me. Twenty-one! Twenty-two! Thereabouts. Boys – *boys*, Winston! Scared for our lives and needing comfort. *Needing love*!' he bellowed, his blue eyes flashing with anger as he crushed his cigarette beneath his boot.

'But *Confusion*,' he continued, 'Confusion with a capital C was mine. To be young and full of love for your bride . . .

To be away at a brutal war and find another love, the kind of thing that creeps up on a man – *unexpectedly*. The kind of thing you don't dare call *love* when *queers* are hated – blackmailed! *And* . . .' he roared, swaying as he ripped off his upper clothes, '. . . plain damn illegal.

'So,' he continued, calming a little as he fumbled out of his trousers and underpants to become fully naked, 'you just *feel* it. The comfort. The companionship of loving eyes. *The unspoken beauty*,' he added softly, making me wish I could have turned the clock back for real and truly helped Ginger and the kids by taking his suffering as my own. Just as quickly, he was barking again, his vulnerable dangly bit whipping from side to side as he staggered this way and that – a passing motorist, the one who'd later tell Bill the Copper that he thought he'd seen a streaker, beeped, enraging him even more.

'Beauty,' he went on, 'beauty that left me squirming with damn guilt. For my marriage . . . for being what I was turning into! And so, *dear* Winston . . .' he suddenly became very still with his arms out flat from his sides and his bearded face thrown right back, '. . . *damn me to Hell for all eternity*, I let him go! Into the abomination of the sea on fire when I could have pulled him to safety. Because *I* was not queer.'

And even though he saluted Sir Winston and clumsily climbed the sea rail, my mind was mostly dizzied by the obvious conclusion that his workshop bullying of Craig was all down to the kid's innocent gay spirit reminding him of the ugliness he'd made of his own queer side. That being the sheer craziness of humans who believe they're cleverer than us dogs, yet who mangle love into violence. And even into death.

80

Way above a blackness so heavy it almost crushed my head, Psycho Vet – who was the emergency call-out – informed Ginger that the severe fits I was having were due to my extremely high temperature, which in turn was caused by distemper; all mutts know that that's usually death with a longer spelling.

Yet I was young Raymond as well as Brucie, my fingers curling away from my special friend as I let the burning ocean take him to where he would always scream my name as his flesh and eyes melted away.

And I was Ginger, whose drunken husband had told her something about the sea being on fire that made her realize at last why he had become an alcoholic: 'My God, Ray, you loved another man on that ship and it was easier to let him go!'

And a fist that I, Raymond, could not keep down flew towards her face, because I was a man and not a queer, and the pain of everything was terrible, and there was blood, blood, blood, and I – for now I was *both* of them – I was the bitch who had provoked it all. At least, according to my worthless, sozzled excuse for a husband, who was always spending money for the family on blasted booze.

But, in fact, I was really only me: Brucie the mangy mutt who was so hot within his darkness he could have grown the coat of an Irish Setter.

And from high, high above, young Rachael came to cuddle me and say that I'd better pull through my 'flipping distemper thing' because her fairy of a twin brother Craig loved me like mad, and if I snuffed it, the family would have to put up with the biggest drama queen on earth. A fond admonishment that at least put gold back into my heart as I waited to die.

81

Then the heat that was making my blood boil became a redness that bore me up into a clear blue sky, where the flapping of a million tiny wings soothed my skin as I was flown past the hard eyes of Sir Winston and out to where the Navy had been doing shell practice before the arrival of the first swarm: the day a year before when Vanessa had got the ladybird up her nose and her dad had helped her.

And, speaking of Raymond, no sooner was I gently released into the cool sea by my kindly red insects than he paddled up, my seal wiggle making me thrash the water because his canoe was an outsize moccasin, and so in a funny way the mystery of where his slippers had gone after he'd left them at the Gay Hussar was now half solved.

'Brucie-Wucie's coming round!' I heard Craig cry. He was speaking from another world, which made me panic and thrash even more.

'He is! He is! Brucie-Wucie's coming round!' he insisted, over a babble of voices. I heard Ginger's distant-seeming advice to Jack, Vanessa and Rachael that they shouldn't get their hopes up as the vet said I was worsening, not improving, like the kid was praying.

'They need you, Bruce,' Raymond called over the noise of my thrashing, his strange canoe bobbing with the movement of the water. 'They need you,' he repeated, as the very last of my energy was spent and I sank to where all was black, but restful in a way I'd never known before.

82

Humans say that dogs sleep with an open eye, but I've only done so on that one occasion when the black was all around and I was so very ill that I was prepared to leave the love of my new family to another mutt that otherwise would have been offed at the municipal kennels.

Ready, that was, except that my right eye became focused on a distant dot of light. As it got nearer it became a ball of silver, within which I saw the furry outline of Her Hoityness padding towards me. She was holding between her teeth the tiny white pup that had been birthed on the fireside rug at the feet of her humans. Too weak to be surprised or delighted that she was coming, I watched as she released her stillborn to where a current took it into the dark. Her brown eyes – immense with the love that only a mother can offer – were fixed upon *me* as she came to lie at my side. 'Drink,' she said, lifting her hind leg to permit easy access to her teats.

'Drink,' she urged as, suddenly, I craved the survival that meant I *would* be there for Ginger and the kids: the dear humans who had brought their love to me that day in the boiling summer of 1976.

ACKNOWLEDGEMENTS

Andreas Campomar and the team at Constable have been a pleasure to work with. In particular I'd like to thank Hazel Orme, whose talent as a copy-editor is second to none. I am eternally grateful to Ian McMillan, Pauline Hadaway and the very special Paul Simpson. Thank you, too, to Jill Clark and Wendy Young for the years of discussion that helped me to find clarity. Other friends and colleagues have been most supportive. They know who they are and I've thanked them elsewhere.